Therapreneur
A therapist's guide to 3x your therapy income
Carly Hill

Carly Hill Coaching LLC

Therapreneur™

How to 3x your therapy income by adding coaching...

Even if you're brand new to business and don't feel quite ready yet.

Cover design by Elijah Toten

Cover photo by Robin Hall, Sand and Sea Studios

This publication is designed to provide factual and helpful information regarding the subject matter covered and from our own client experiences. It is sold with the understanding that the publisher is not engaged in rendering legal, accounting, or other professional services. If you require legal advice or other expert assistance, you should seek the services of a competent individual.

Disclaimer: The author makes no guarantees to the results you'll achieve by reading this book. All business requires risk and hard work. The results and client case studies presented in this book represent results achieved working directly with the authorities. Your results may vary when undertaking any new business venture or marketing strategy.

E-Book Edition ISBN: 979-8-9879086-1-7

Paperback Edition ISBN: 979-8-9879086-0-0

Audio Edition ISBN: 979-8-9879086-2-4

To every therapist who got this special calling to help others, your work is priceless.

Who Are We?

Therapreneurs™ are a new breed of clinicians; they are ambitious and shift the dynamic of the helping field.

They expand beyond the therapy couch and are changing lives all over the world, sharing their God given gifts and skills bravely and using their creativity to help others heal.

Why? Therapreneurs™ are different.

Their mission is much bigger than the box licensing boards have put them in. Therapreneurs™ leverage their time because they know their knowledge is priceless and they refuse to settle with outdated industry standards.

Impact is their middle name. They diversify their skill set, never hold back, and they love taking risks knowing it's going to positively contribute to someone's life.

Therapreneurs™ embody and model a balanced life because they know it's impossible to pour from an empty cup.

Therapreneurs™ have time for themselves and their family. They have an abundance of what is truly valuable to them, and they can do what they want to do when they want to do it. They have complete control over their lives.

Burnout is not in their vocabulary.

Therapreneurs™ are genuine badasses, operating their dream business with multiple streams of income while sharing their genius with the world and completing their life's purpose to help and heal as many lives as possible!

Dear Therapist,

I am thrilled to be writing this letter to you, as it means you have taken the time to pick up my book with the intention of turning your desire and passion to help others into a thriving business. Congratulations on taking the first step towards starting and growing a successful coaching business!

As a fellow Therapreneur™, I understand the challenges you face daily when it comes to helping clients achieve their goals while taking care of yourself and family. I also understand the challenges of starting and scaling a business. However with the right tools and strategies, anyone can build a successful coaching business and make a positive impact in the lives of their clients.

I wrote this book to provide you with the information, guidance, and inspiration you need to start and grow a successful coaching business. This book will allow you to make a bigger impact while simultaneously finding greater freedom and fulfillment in your own life. It's a win-win.

In these pages, you will find a collection of strategies and approaches that have been proven to be effective in helping ambitious therapists expand beyond the therapy couch and find a sense of liberation and peace once and for all.

Guidance from differentiating therapy and coaching, protecting your license, developing a unique coaching niche, creating a strong brand, and marketing and delivering your services effectively is all here.

I hope that as you read this book and implement these techniques, you will find a greater sense of personal and professional fulfillment and be able to make a bigger impact in the lives of your clients.

Thank you for choosing to join me on this journey towards greater freedom. I am confident that you will find the information and tools in this book to be valuable and transformative.

Let's get started! I can't wait to see what you'll achieve.

Please join the Therapist to Coach Accelerator™ Facebook™ group for FREE video trainings on every topic discussed within these pages.

XOXO Carly

Forward

"It takes years as a woman to unlearn what you have been taught to be sorry for."   -Amy Poehler

We have been conditioned as women:

- To behave a certain way

- To be quiet and not ask for what we want

- To work tirelessly for dirt money

- To not charge too much

- To give freely without the expectation of compensation

And that having it all means doing it all.

That is a lie.

If we have been conditioned, it means we can be deconditioned.

There are too many genius women hiding their expertise and experience because they are living in fear.

Many of us are afraid of what people will think of us if we act on our desire.

We are afraid we will put time and effort into our business, and it will fail.

Not to mention we think we must do it all by ourselves.

So many of us think we don't know enough yet and what we have to offer isn't good enough.

We undervalue our knowledge and think people don't need our support.

In reality, people are leaning on us constantly.

Our own fear and doubt leave us settling for less than our true value.

We continue to dream but our dreams are "one-day" thoughts.

If you can relate to any of this, I want you to know that this is all about to change.

It's about to change because you are reading this book and your one-day thought is now becoming day one.

Today is day one of you owning your power, standing in your power, and putting tape over the mouth of your voice of self-doubt.

Making confident decisions, embracing bravery, taking a leap of faith, and acknowledging your intuitive abilities starts now.

Let's do this, ladies!

Contents

There are 2 reasons this book exists:

1. I'd love for you to eventually invest in the Therapist to Coach Accelerator™ program so you have the support you need to implement everything inside this book.

2. To empower you to start achieving now so you'll understand the true value of #1 and take action as soon as possible.

You will soon find out that I'm obsessed with giving away free valuable content and if you are in the Therapist to Coach Accelerator Facebook™ community, you probably already know that.

My colleagues think I'm crazy for doing so but I don't hold back. I've been on the struggle bus, and this is my way of paying it forward so you don't have to.

I'm going to help you right here, right now!

PS: If at any time throughout this book, you feel ready to schedule a no cost strategy call to lay out your exact coaching blueprint then head on over to www.carlyhillcoaching.com

Introduction

From a very young age, I always knew I wanted to help people. I grew up in a small Florida town just outside of Orlando with one older brother and 2 loving parents. We were an average middle class working family. My dad was an arborist who owned his own company, and my mom was either working as a teacher, social worker, or staying at home with my brother and I. I went to Catholic school for 9 years, was always involved in extracurricular activities and sports, and was spoiled to say the least.

I had a great childhood and my parents made sure I knew how fortunate I was. They would often take me to volunteer in the community and I vividly remember wearing my little girl scout vest as I was bringing the homeless blankets or taking meals to a rest home. Although, I'm sure I would have rather spent my time outside climbing trees or playing with friends, I'm incredibly blessed that I grew up with a good head on my shoulders and a giving spirit. I knew I wanted to keep giving.

As a child, the only thing I could conceptualize was wanting to be a teacher. I remember lining up all my stuffed animals in my bright yellow and purple room and teaching them God knows what from my mini whiteboard. I loved being in charge, pointing at things, and typically I was photographed with one hand on my hip. My parents gave me the nickname "sassafras" because I always seemed to have an opinion. I like to think I was just a natural born leader with spunk.

But seriously, my teachers were my idols and I wanted to be just like them when I grew up. I also adored any child younger than me and started babysitting much younger than I probably should have. I remember printing and cutting my own homemade babysitting business cards and putting them in the neighborhood mailboxes. I guess I was a mini entrepreneur too! The combination of my love for children, even though I was one, and teaching made it easy for me to decide I was going to be a schoolteacher when I grew up.

I was set on this all the way up until my sophomore year of college when I had to officially pick my major before wasting my time taking a bunch of classes that wouldn't help me graduate. My current major at the time was early childhood education, which I loved, but I had an itch to do more. I wanted to teach kids more than their ABC's. I wanted to get deep into their life story and help them. Maybe I got that from my mom. She was my role model too, so it only seemed natural to follow in her social work path.

So, I started to look into it with my career counselor and it made perfect sense to me. It's embarrassing for me to admit, but the real deal breaker was when the counselor told me I didn't even have to take math to become a social worker. I said, "sign me up". Clearly, I was in my element though because I started getting straight As in all my social work classes. I was in love with what I was learning, and I was excited to make a difference. I followed all the way through to my master's degree and before I knew it, I was officially a therapist.

On my first day as a therapist, I was so invigorated. I was a bit overwhelmed by being thrown into the actual work, but I was excited to help people and make an impact. I was working in a community mental health agency along with many other "newbie" therapists. We each carried a caseload of about 25+ clients and we were responsible for fitting them all into our schedule each week.

Each morning, I would get up and put on my business professional outfit before starting my day. From there, I'd pull out my map, which felt more like a 1000-piece puzzle, and point myself toward my first appointment. I kept my "office" in my car and would eat lunch in front of my steering wheel between back-to-back sessions. I provided therapy on car hoods, in Denny's parking lots, and in schools and strangers' homes. It was definitely sketchy at times.

When I did return to the office to complete my paperwork and update my notes, there were 30 desks smashed into the same room under old-school, yellow, florescent lighting with 5 supervisor offices surrounding us. Their offices had doors, but we did not. I'd usually try to snag a seat next to the window where I could get some vitamin D and a view of the dingy parking lot. It was my best option.

This was my life for over two years, but it felt more like five. My experience was incredible and my confidence as a therapist was boosted tremendously. After two years, I felt like I had seen it all. However, it wasn't sustainable. I was traveling all over the county, scheduling and seeing 25+ clients a week, and trying to keep up with paperwork all while being paid $18 per hour with a master's degree.

It was madness to say the least and I was extremely burnt out. My tank was so empty that I was stoked when I got a no show. Only then could I breathe for a second. I would usually take myself to TJ Max for some retail therapy when I had a last-minute cancellation or no show; it was much needed. I was hanging on by a thread because I knew better opportunities would open up for me once I got my license. I couldn't wait.

Although I had already graduated, I felt like I was still in school. My official title was a registered intern, which felt insulting, and I was working my way towards completing 1,500+ hours of clinical work and 100+ hours of supervision. I was ready to be an officially licensed therapist already.

After meeting my clinical hours and spending countless hours studying, I was finally ready to take my clinical exam for licensure. I remember the day I took the test like it was yesterday. I ate the healthiest breakfast I could, drove to my test center, placed all my belongings in my locker, and walked into the test taking room with my head held high. I used all the allotted 4 hours and ended up passing by 6 points. I was never good at taking tests and this was an extremely hard one.

When I walked out of the room and the lady behind the desk passed me the paper that said, pass, I let out a big sigh and was incredibly relieved. I immediately rode the elevator down to the first floor to go outside and call anyone and everyone I could to tell them I passed. I was jumping with excitement and was looking forward to celebrating with an extra dirty martini with blue cheese olives, my favorite. I knew I was on the right track to bigger and better things.

After a weekend of celebrating, I went back into the office and immediately marched myself to HR to set up an appointment to discuss a pay raise. I deserved it. If you have ever been in community mental health, I'm sure you could probably guess how this was about to go for me.

The next day, my clinical director, supervisor, and myself all sat down in the clinical director's office. They knew why I was there. They congratulated me for passing and immediately stated that as much as they would love to be able to offer me more, their budget only allows for a $2 per hour raise. I had no words. A whopping $2 raise, are you kidding me? At the time of writing this, I still don't have words. I just knew I had to find a way out. When you are in the wrong place, you start to look around for the right place and I thought I had found it, but I wasn't sure how I was going to attain it.

My previous and most favorite supervisor, Tina, had left a few months prior to work at a brain performance center. One morning when we were getting breakfast and catching up, I started begging her to help me get a job there. It was truly my dream job at the time. I had always been fascinated by the neurological side of things plus I'd have better pay, be able to park my car and go into an office, and it was only a five-minute commute from my house. I had my mind made up. I needed and wanted this job. She put in a good word for me, and I immediately applied.

The director wanted to bring me on but there wasn't room at the time. I ended up interviewing seven months prior to starting and waited and waited until the position was available. I wanted the job that bad. In the meantime, I continued to put my big girl pants on and show up to my current job with a smile on my face. It was only a matter of time before I'd be out of there.

Sure enough, I finally got the phone call with the offer. It was the same exact day I put in my two weeks' notice at my community mental health agency and let's just say I've never had a bigger smile than the day I drove out of that dingy parking lot. I truly knew I was on to bigger and better things.

My first day on the job at the brain performance center was amazing. It was a night and day difference from community mental health. The office had a nice, modern, and clean feel with updated equipment and a well-stocked water and coffee station. We had one large conference table for our small team of eight in the back, many offices to choose from when we were seeing individual clients, and a massive movie theater room full of individual TV stations for clients to complete their neurofeedback brain training. The company bought us all lunch as a celebration of my first day and I immediately bonded with the team who already felt more like family. I left work that day feeling on top of the world.

I loved the work I continued to do there. It's hard for me to describe how cool it was as a therapist to be able to scan a client's brain and understand why they were presenting with the symptoms they were and be able to treat them naturally. Plus, I got to scan and treat my own brain for free too. We would even have some professional athletes come in from time to time to work on their peak performance. Like I said, it was just an overall cool job.

However, as years went on, cool wasn't seeming to cut it anymore. I was secretly suffering. I did love my job, I loved my team, and I loved the work I was doing but I was still a broke psychotherapist living in burnout land.

There I was, four years post grad, still pouring my blood, sweat, and tears into a job that didn't recognize my worth. I wasn't even making $50,000 a year. It's sad because at the time, I remember telling my now husband that there are no other options for me. He never agreed but I truly couldn't see a way out. I thought I couldn't do any better. I also thought starting my own business would be way too hard, even though it was always a goal. In social work school they warn you that you have to pay your dues first and despite how twisted that was, I had subconsciously absorbed it. I was settling.

I didn't have the freedom, security, and flexibility that I always dreamed of, which crushed me because freedom was always something I valued highly. This seems incredibly irresponsible, and it probably was but I would quit jobs in college if they didn't give me the time off that I needed. I knew my friends, family, and memories were more important and that I could always get a new job if I needed to.

Now, I wouldn't dare quit my career job because I couldn't get time off and I usually always did when I needed it, but I still felt trapped. I still didn't have the freedom I was craving. I'd stare out the window thinking about how I could be working out, running errands, and doing work on my own time instead of someone else telling me what and when I had to do it.

I also had a burning desire for financial freedom and would often google side hustles so I could leverage my time when I wasn't busy at work. At one point I had three jobs at once because I had picked up two side hustles to leverage my time and make more money.

I knew this wasn't the life for me, but I didn't know what steps to take. I didn't have an exit strategy and it was scary to even think about one. So, I settled.

BUT the universe said NOPE. No settling for you Carly. "You're laid off."

It was an odd feeling of calm and confusion the day my company told us all on Zoom. None of us saw this happening at all. We were all laid off. It seemed completely out of the blue to hear the company was shutting down indefinitely, but I guess they were one of the many companies who were impacted by the pandemic. As I took a deep breath, I subconsciously knew I was going to be okay, but I had no idea what was about to happen. I had never been laid off before. The type A planner in me did not like not having a plan.

I wish I could sit here and tell you I laid down my foot and said, enough is enough and I'm doing the damn thing, and that's how I started my entrepreneurial journey but that simply was not the case. I was kind of thrown into it. Along with a ton of self-doubt, sleepless nights, and honestly, thoughts about applying for jobs again.

I distinctly remember sitting at the dining room table staring blankly at my laptop thinking I had two choices:

1. Start searching for a new job.

Or

2. Put the metal to the freaking pedal and blast off in private practice.

Bravely, I chose the second and it was scary as hell. I had no clue what I was doing but I knew I could figure it out eventually. In hindsight, losing my job was the best thing that ever happened to me and the exact push I needed but at the same time, all I could feel was fear as I stepped into my entrepreneurial journey.

My biggest concern was money, so I frantically signed up as a better help therapist where I got paid $35 a session. Any therapist knows that this is a total last resort. It was a complete joke and I think I lasted two months. My focus was back on full time private practice.

I was attempting to make all the right moves, but I was questioning everything I did. I kept telling myself the story of "I'm just a social worker, not a businesswoman" and it was leaving me with a full plate of self-doubt. I remember doing a solo yoga session in my backyard to release the fear and the tears were just streaming down my face. I was so scared of the unknown. My ego was getting the best of me; it's good like that.

Looking back, the whole process of starting private practice was quite chaotic. I was constantly back tracking and overpaying for systems. I felt like I was always doing busy work, but I can't tell you what direction it was pointing me in. I was Youtubing, podcasting, and annoying the crap out of other therapists just so I could learn all things marketing, messaging, sales, and business.

I was discouraged to say the least. I thought private practice was supposed to be my way to freedom. Instead, I was left with a ton of admin and busy work, an inconsistent revenue stream, a whisper of a voice, and a lack of freedom.

However, I will say I loved working from home in my sweatpants and being able to change the laundry in between my back-to-back sessions. That was my glimpse of freedom.

Private practice just wasn't the dream I had always made it out to be in my mind. It was a whole lot easier when I figured out the business side of things, but I was still only getting paid when my butt was in the therapy chair and only after I saw a client. The only way I knew how to make more money was to take more clients, but I didn't have the mental capacity to do so.

I had a full caseload from my warm network and as it was, I hardly had any time for myself, family, or friends. Yet, I still had an itch to make a bigger impact. Nothing was adding up. I was over it and it was an agonizing feeling. I even wrote a poem about it.

To put it into perspective, I was basically questioning my whole career as a therapist. I was thinking, "this life is not sustainable."

I remember waking up in the morning sometimes and saying to myself, "Ugh, I don't feel like being a therapist today."

I attempted to hire business coaches to show me the way to having a sustainable practice. Unfortunately, all I seemed to land on were money-hungry coaches who left me feeling jaded or coaches who promised me strategy but only spoke about mindset instead.

I knew there had to be a better way. A way that wasn't stressful. A way that gave me plenty of freedom, security, and flexibility while simultaneously changing people's lives.

Amid my frustrations, I had a massive realization that I wasn't even doing therapy with clients in my practice. I was actually coaching them instead. This seems like a silly realization and something I probably should have known, but the truth is there are so many nuances between therapy and coaching. It can often be a really confusing distinction, especially when you are so used to only identifying with your therapist role.

I was a coach because I was working with non-clinical problems, yet I was still limiting the lives I could impact due to the archaic interjurisdictional licensure limitations. It didn't seem right.

Yet, it also didn't fully feel right calling myself a coach after I worked so hard for my therapy license. Full transparency, I would roll my eyes at coaches thinking everyone and their mom was a coach, and they were just "want-to-be" therapists. However, I was also curious.

I saw how successful they were and thought maybe they knew something we didn't.

I thought it was because they had a coaching certification and had some superpower fast way of getting clients' results. I learned their success was due to the proven business strategies they were following and how specific they were in who they helped and how they helped them. This is something that can be totally foreign to a therapist who is used to solving every problem under the sun.

I knew I needed to dive into this deeper because all these thoughts left me with one big burning question. How can I ethically change lives nationwide while also earning back my freedom? To be more clear, how can I be both a therapist and a coach, protect my license, and leverage my time so I can finally get paid for my knowledge?

I needed to know but I was scared to invest in coaches and programs again knowing it didn't turn out for me so well the first time. On top of that, I was deep diving into my own spiritual journey and realized my disserving money beliefs were also contributing to my fear of investing in mentorship. Long story short, I did a lot of inner work and got past them.

With a determined mind, I set off on my mission and invested in multiple high ticket business programs and organic lead generation trainings to understand what was sustainable for agents of change. When I would tell people that I invested $5,000-$10,000 multiple times to be in coaching programs, they thought I was crazy, but it was starting to be my new normal. It was always worth it. I was on a mission, and nothing could stop me. I kept telling my friends, "I'm going to crack the code this time, watch me!"

I can't tell you how many nights I stayed up until three AM consuming any piece of helpful information I could get my hands on. I was obsessed, but in a good way. I pretty much stopped listening to music and replaced it with audiobooks and podcasts. I was so fascinated that I never wanted to stop learning and with all the information out there I knew I wouldn't. Understanding marketing, business, lead generation, and sales was a whole new world to me, and I couldn't get enough of it. It was all starting to make sense.

I also spoke to multiple attorneys in the coaching space to understand the nuances between therapy and coaching and how one could protect their license as they dove into the coaching world. I was on a mission to piece this all together.

In hindsight, I'm very grateful for my early struggles because it's exactly what led me to my love for marketing and business and understanding all things coaching. This journey has helped me grow as a uniquely positioned business coach. I never ever thought I'd end up in this role. I'm a social worker by trade, and as you know, we don't learn shit about business in graduate school, but I've lived the relatable life that your typical business coach would never be able to understand.

- Being overworked and underpaid in community mental health

- Seeing back-to-back clients and having no time to pee

- Feeling desperate for more money and picking up shifts on Better Help

- Wondering why no one is finding me and asking myself if I should switch careers

- Fighting insurance companies and doing unnecessary admin work on my unpaid time

- Rolling my eyes at clients expecting me to be cheap, free, or covered by their co-pay

- Having a packed schedule and no time for family, friends, or self-care

- Feeling hopeless and confused in my inability to grow my business

I have been there, in every single one of those places and it's a huge part of why I started this business. I don't want you to have to go through the same trial and error that I did.

If you'd like to expedite your results, please contact me and my team. We'd love to help you streamline the process. You can schedule your no cost strategy session at www.carlyhillcoaching.com

I knew success was possible. I knew I needed to get to the place of leveraging my time to match my lifestyle. I knew it was possible to make more money, I saw people doing it.

So, I kept pushing, kept trying, kept investing, and kept trusting. Then BOOM, I finally cracked the code. I had all the information I needed to answer the burning question of what was sustainable for agents of change.

What I discovered was mind blowing, so mind blowing that it became my new mission to teach it to any clinician suffering the way I had been.

It was an unforeseen but easy transition for me to move into full time business coaching for therapists. I deeply believe and always say that we are here to learn what we are most meant to teach. I had to walk myself through it so I could then guide other ambitious, driven, and intentional therapists. The ones who are ready to level up and impact more lives. The ones who are ready to outgrow the office and live a sustainable lifestyle. The ones who have an open mind and are ready to leave behind the outdated model of mental health.

The mental health system is broken in more than one way and so many clinicians are ready to throw the towel in and quit. They are even thinking about leaving the mental health field completely. I see conversations like this happening all the time. They are burnt out and rightfully so! The demand for care is so high but the therapists are overworked and underpaid. Insurance isn't reimbursing enough or takes too long to do so. They have loans to pay and a family to tend to. The list goes on and on.

It breaks my heart to see clinicians hurting and lacking sustainability, knowing that we are approximately 1.8 million therapists short of what's needed to efficiently treat mental illness. However, I know firsthand the struggle of wanting to throw the towel in. I started a local networking group just to help therapists beat burnout for this reason. The idea came to me one day after yoga while showering. Who doesn't get the best ideas in the shower? I had a visual in my head of a bunch of therapists chatting it up over snacks and wine. Inspiring one another, lifting each other up, sharing stories, and beating burnout. I immediately texted my therapist friend, Olivia, and told her about the idea. We didn't even think twice and knew we had to execute this idea. Therapists needed this. We needed this. A safe space to vent and let go that didn't feel like a "work" event. We immediately got to work and collaborated with an event planning company that specializes in paradise picnics. I also went on Canva and quickly created a brand kit so I could create a social media account. We were starting before we were ready, and we were just rolling with the punches.

We had a soft opening with nine therapists, including us, and we had a blast. We laughed, we cried, we ate, we drank, we inspired one another and ultimately everyone left with their heart full, ready to give back to their clients. Not to mention, the aesthetics were on point, thanks to our picnic queen, Phoebe! These Therapists Unite events have blown up and turned into more than I could have ever imagined. It warms my heart knowing that we've created a space for all local healers involved in the advanced mental, physical, and spiritual health realm. This just goes to show, it only takes a shower thought to get something started!

Therapists Unite was only one of my creations when it came to helping therapists live a sustainable life and it was more of a passion project than anything. The one thing I really knew I needed to do was take all the marketing and business knowledge I had learned, along with my own experience of traveling this journey myself and share it with other therapists.

So, I did exactly that. I spent three months building out an online course to help therapists add coaching, protect their license, and create, market, and sell their very own signature coaching program. One that would help them make a bigger impact while also earning back their freedom.

I named it the Therapist to Coach Accelerator™.

At the time of writing this, I am proud to say that I have had the pleasure of guiding many clinicians, in many different countries, through the Therapist to Coach Accelerator™ program successfully. I've never met more supportive women in my life. It's truly a sisterhood we have. A Therapreneur™ tribe!

It's an incredible feeling to be able to have flexibility, sustainability, and security in my life while simultaneously teaching others how they can achieve it too. I get paid even when I sleep at night. I have time for myself, family and friends like never before and I'm impacting even more lives because I can work with people all around the world.

To put it into perspective, what used to take me a whole year to make, now only takes me a month. I wake up every morning excited to start my day. I'm passionate about what I'm doing. I have the flexibility I've always dreamed of. I have the security of knowing my family's financial goals will be met. Most importantly, I have the freedom to create my own destiny.

It is with these goals in mind that I write this book. I want to provide a clear and actionable plan for therapists so that they can feel freedom too. Freedom with knowing they are impacting more lives as well as location freedom, financial freedom, and time freedom. Something every agent of change deserves.

This book will go over the exact steps a therapist needs to take in order to call themselves a coach, protect their license, and create, market, and sell their signature coaching program at a high-ticket price so they can make three times their therapy income and impact more lives.

Chapter 1

Transition from Therapist to Coach

I teach you the difference between therapy and coaching and how to add coaching ethically and legally so you insure you are protecting your hard-earned license and have the peace of mind that you are setting up your business the right way.

All therapists face a unique challenge when it comes to legality and ethics when adding a coaching aspect to their business. It's important to look for foreseeable conflicts that can create misunderstandings and sticky situations that would lead to hearings before the ethics committee, loss of licensure, or lawsuits. I don't say this to scare you and certainly don't want you spending your days freaking out about your next pitfall. I say it to be real and to pop the question in your head, "How can I do this the right way?" I want you to have the peace of mind that you are adding coaching the correct way and protecting your hard-earned license. If I'm being honest, it's pretty difficult to land yourself in deep trouble unless you're just being ignorant.

I will be focusing on psychotherapists in this book, but any licensed practitioner should take the necessary precautions to ensure they are abiding by the ethical and legal standards of their field. A lot of the same concepts apply to all licensed therapists. Consulting with a lawyer is best practice.

No one makes this massive shift or change without a strong purpose or reason.

I'm curious why you are here. I mean, clearly you are interested in tripling your therapy income and adding coaching, but I'd love to know why. I'd encourage you to reflect on this right now. Use the following questions to help you outline your *why* for being here:

- Do you feel limited by your license, location, or even your career options?

- Do you feel limited by the people you can work with or how much money you can make?

- Do you resonate more with a coaching style?

- Do you enjoy working with more situational and less severe problems?

- Do you not like diagnosing people?

- Are you feeling burnt out?

- Are you sick of insurance?

- Do you wish you had more time with family or friends?

- Do you wish you could pay back your loans or save more?

- Do you have an itch to grow but don't know how?

Whatever your **why** is, it's important. Staying grounded in your why will always help you move forward into uncharted territory, especially when it gets challenging.

I want you to know that whatever roadblock, limitation, challenge, or fear you are feeling right now, it's totally okay. If you are reading this book, you have a desire to break free, and that says a ton about you and where you are going. You have so many skills and gifts, and I'm going to help you be seen for them. Not everyone gets this calling to be an agent of change, but you did. People are waiting, wishing, and praying for you right now. I want to help you add coaching so you can impact more lives and add multiple revenue streams into your life. This is going to be life-changing.

I also want you to know that if you are here to learn about coaching with the intention of adding it, you never have to stop doing therapy. You don't lose your title of a therapist when you gain your bonus identity of a coach. It's both, not one or the other.

There is a time and place for therapy and a time and place for coaching. The beautiful thing is you can do both. Therapists can be coaches, but coaches can't just be therapists.

So, let's dive into the nuances of therapy and coaching. Shall we?

One of the biggest questions I get is "What is the difference?"

Perhaps you have Googled the difference before and felt even more confused, or maybe you have gathered a bunch of different answers from a bunch of different people, and you don't know who to believe. I totally understand, and not to worry, I'm going to give you the easiest definition in the world. You can adapt this as your own right now.

Therapy is working with medical necessity. Coaching is not. To explain further, therapy is working with medical necessity while coaching is working with more situational, less severe problems.

That's it!!

For example, a client is having panic attacks and has agoraphobia. They require therapy. A client is nervous taking their kids to the park or gets sweats in large social settings. They require coaching.

Another clarifying example would be if a client is having flashbacks from a domestic violent relationship, they will need therapy. If a client is heartbroken and is having trouble grieving breakup, they will require coaching.

Can you see the difference? Now, I'm sure you could argue that everyone and their mom, including us, could meet criteria for some sort of diagnosis, especially if you looked through our big purple bible long enough. Right? I'm the first one to admit that I have handed out the adjustment disorder diagnosis in the past. Maybe you have too, but that is not the point I'm trying to make here.

The point is, as a therapist, you are treating a diagnosis and in coaching, you are not. You need to use your clinical discernment. You are the clinician, and you get to decide whether they are a fit for coaching or a fit for therapy, not the client. Although the stigma has gotten a lot better these days some people can still only fathom getting help under the umbrella of coaching, when in reality, they are meeting textbook DSM criteria and need therapy. Now, I don't want to confuse you, but it is very possible for a client to be meeting criteria for a diagnosis and still come into your coaching program. What it really comes down to is this, are you treating them for medical necessity or not?

For example, I worked with a therapist-turned-coach who created a signature coaching program for women who have come out of toxic relationships. A lot of her clients were meeting criteria for PTSD. However, she was not treating them for PTSD. Her coaching program was strictly to help them boost their self-confidence and get back into the dating world. A lot of her clients had their own therapist to work through their PTSD, and they simultaneously were in her coaching program to boost their confidence and get back into the dating world. It was very specific to the situational problem they had.

It's important to note that you should not transfer one of your own clients from therapy to coaching or coaching to therapy. This is considered a dual relationship. In social work, once a client, always a client. Whereas LPC's and LMFT's have a statute of limitations, where after two years, it's fair game. It's important not to switch a therapy client into a coaching client because it can be hard for your clients to unsee you as their therapist. The best practice is to check with your board if you ever feel confused.

Now, one could also argue that if a therapy client did so much work with you that they are no longer meeting criteria for a diagnosis, or rather, you are no longer treating them for medical necessity, then aren't you technically coaching? All I have to say is, I didn't make the rules. (insert eye roll)

Let's re-focus on the nuances between the two because it can be confusing.

The biggest one I disagree with is, therapy focuses on the past and present and coaching focuses on the present and future. While I understand it, I also think that most therapists and coaches would agree that the past, present and future is discussed in both a coaching and therapy relationship. I do agree that therapy is usually for a longer period of time and coaching is usually for a set period or short time, but this is also dependent on the type of therapeutic modality being used.

We all know and can agree on the fact that the therapy field is regulated, and the coaching field is not. From what I have seen, most state licensing boards do not require you to get a coaching certification. By all means, if you want one or it will make you feel confident, I say go for it but in my opinion, therapists make the best coaches and therapists already know how to coach. It's simply solving a non-clinical problem. I deem you a coach right now!

I often see therapists getting all worked up about not knowing if they are doing therapy or doing coaching. Just remember, it goes back to the severity of the issue the client is having. Are you treating them for medical necessity or not?

In coaching, you can even use therapy modalities if you aren't treating medical necessity. When we hear CBT for example, we automatically think of therapy, but I dare you right now to Google CBT coaching certification. There is a coaching certification for just about every therapeutic modality we have been trained in. There is even EMDR coaching. Crazy, right? I hope I'm opening your eyes here. All this information sure was an eye opener for me. Correct me if I'm wrong but I often feel like we are so tied to our therapist title, because that is what we are by trade, that we forget how much we truly can do. The world is our oyster, y'all. We have lives to change.

Coaches have much more flexibility and freedom in how they treat their clients. I always loved this as a coach because I was able to weave in all my woo-woo stuff anytime I wanted. Not to say that it's not possible to include some of your out-of-the-box passions in your therapy practice, because you totally can. But if you market yourself as a therapist, and say "come to my meditation somatic workshop because I'm a therapist," then you have to act like a therapist in terms of confidentiality, testimonial rules, paperwork, etc. With that being said, I think it's important to decide if you are going to be billing services, such as workshops, under your therapy practice or if you want a second business where you can play around outside the limits of your board and be billing services under that coaching title.

All of that brings me to my next point. Even as a coach it's very important to understand that you are still held to your ethics. Your coaching contract should always have mandated reporting and informed consent. If you have both a private practice and a coaching business, your private practice paperwork should state that you provide services outside the scope of therapy, but the client is under no obligation to purchase said services or products and that they have no bearing on the outcome of therapy. It's important to release this power differential and let them know they are under no obligation to purchase something. Examples of this would be if you had workshops, retreats, sold oils or other products, etc. Clients wouldn't need to purchase your essential oils in order to get results, but they very well may want to. Just ensure that you aren't crossing the ethical guideline of a dual relationship. It can get confusing here. This is why lawyers exist for therapists-turned-coaches specifically. Most of them already have paperwork bundles for these types of scenarios.

If you do have a coaching business in addition to your private practice, you should maintain professional liability insurance. It's sometimes known as errors and omissions. The rule of thumb, when it comes to protecting your license, is to keep everything separate. Separate business entities, bank accounts, insurance, clients, and marketing. It's not as hard as you think. I know it can sound intimidating to have two of everything, but once it's set up it's done, you have the peace of mind that you did it the right way. It's always best practice to consult with your board, too, and let them know what you are doing. We know that rules can vary across state lines, which drives me crazy, but you can never be too careful so it's worth it to do your due diligence.

Just because your friend slapped coaching on their private practice website without taking the steps to protect their license or liability doesn't mean you should too. I'm sure you've also seen therapists who use coaching as a loophole to see clients out of state when, in reality, they are meeting medical necessity and should truly be therapy clients. Let's set a better example.

It's my hope that this chapter helped you understand the difference between therapy and coaching and the steps you need to take to protect your hard-earned license. Just know that support is available when it comes to this somewhat tedious process of separating everything out.

You transform lives for a living; you can totally handle the steps you need to take when it comes to transitioning or adding coaching ethically and legally. It's worth it, trust me.

Recap:

I deem you a coach right now; just make sure you protect your license!

Remember, you don't lose your therapist identity. You just gained a bonus identity!

Therapists can be coaches, but coaches can't be therapists.

Join the Therapist to Coach Accelerator™ Facebook™ group to download the therapist to coach checklist that will show you exactly how to protect your license.

Chapter 2

Riches are in the Niches

You will learn how to set up your online coaching blueprint and select a viable and marketable coaching niche so you can confidently say exactly who you help and how you help them.

Picking a niche can be foreign to us. When I worked in community mental health, I was helping 4-year-olds, 14-year-olds, and 40-year-olds. I was all over the place with the problems I was solving and the people I was helping. When I took insurance in private practice, I was all over the place too. My incoming clients felt like a box of chocolates; I never knew what I was going to get. I was basically solving every problem under the sun and just morphing into whoever I needed to be in order to help the person sitting in front of me. Of course, I had my favorite types of clients and clients I was extra excited to see, but it felt out of reach to get *only* these types of clients. It seemed more like the luck of the draw when I did end up with a good bunch on my caseload.

When I got more serious and decided I was going to niche down to call in more of these soulmate clients, I had a big problem.

I had no idea how to articulate what my ideal clients' pains, desires, and needs were. I was going too broad because that is what I knew. I had an itch to save the world and my website was full of platitudes or cliches like, "live your best life", "manifest a reality you love", "unlock your potential", "feel happy and confident again", "get clarity." Something any therapist or coach could probably say.

I also talked about my process a lot because that is how I loved to help. It was my baby and something I firmly believed in. I was probably using clinical words too and listing the zillion certifications I had because that's what I saw other therapists doing. I realize now that we were just all probably trying to impress one another. I've come to know that people don't care about our process, our credentials, and certainly not our clinical jargon. They just need to like us, trust us, and know that we can solve their problem. That's it.

It's safe to say, when I tried to niche down, I was falling on deaf ears and it was agonizing. Here are exact quotes from a poem I wrote as I sat in my car one day feeling defeated with my mission to impact more lives.

I have so much gold to offer, so much so it's scattered all over the place.

A field of 4 leaf clovers in too big of a space.

An itch to help the world with a whisper of a voice.

I did not understand market demand or copywriting. All I had was a big ole heart and a half-ass plan I believed in. The bottom line is, you need demand for your service to work. This means you are looking for a starving crowd.

A marketing professor asked his students, "If you were going to open a hot dog stand, and you could only have one advantage over your competitors, which would it be?"

"Location! Quality! Low prices! Best taste!" The students kept going until eventually they had run out of answers.

They looked at each other waiting for the professor to speak. The room finally fell quiet.

The professor smiled and replied, "A starving crowd."

You could have the worst hot dogs, terrible prices, and be in a terrible location, but if you're the only hot dog stand in town and the local college football game breaks out, you're going to sell out. That's the value of a starving crowd. (Hormozi, 2021)

Think about the toilet paper shortage when the pandemic hit. Toilet paper was flying off the shelves without an offer, but the crowd was hungry.

Fundamental Decisions

Having clarity about who you help, how you help them, and what makes you different is incredibly important. It's essentially the foundation of your business. And in order to have a strong foundation, fundamental decisions need to be made. None of these decisions are permanent. I don't want this to scare you. We can always go back and refine.

Let's begin sketching out the blueprint for your coaching business. This is going to be fun because your coaching business is not only about achieving financial freedom. It's also about personal fulfillment and reflecting the true and unique value that only you can deliver and then getting really clear on what that is. Exciting, right?

So, let's start with discussing your coaching title and the industry you'll fall under. The following industries meet fundamental human needs and I guarantee you'll fall under one of these categories. Health, wealth, and relationships are the three biggest markets and what keeps people up at night. When someone is lacking in one of these three areas, tremendous pain exists. It's just how we are wired.

- Health & Wellness (mental or physical, fitness, weight loss, sleep, auto immune, stress, burnout, loneliness, empowerment, healing)

- Money & Business (wealth, entrepreneurship, coaching, consulting)

- Relationships (marriage, divorce, dating, God, spirit, self, family, parents/kids, friends)

Most therapists will probably fall under the health and wellness or relationship category but as you can see, options are endless.

I've even seen therapists combine their passion for music and arts with health and wellness or combine wealth and mental health in helping people clear money blocks energetically.

You'll also want a coaching title. Options are endless here too. Here are some ideas.

- Life Coach

- Parent Coach

- Embodiment Coach

- Resilience Coach

- Christian Coach

- Perinatal Coach

- Breakup Coach

- Dating Coach

- Fitness Coach

- Weight Loss Coach

- Self-Love Coach

- Relationship Coach

- Women Empowerment Coach

- Sleep Coach

- Business Coach

It's important to be clear and concise with your title. This is not the place to get cutesy and clever.

Now that you know your industry and title, it's time to get a bit more granular with who you help and how you help them.

Notice how I didn't say anything about your process or the modalities you use? Your niche is not those things. As therapists, we do tend to talk about our how a lot. It's what we are trained and passionate about, but we can't mistake that for our outcome or our niche. Transformational healing, trauma, stress, or EMDR is not a niche.

Try filling in this statement below to find your niche.

- I help (population) achieve/solve (result/problem) so that (biggest benefit, desired outcome-life changing result-big goal)

Here are some examples:

I help expecting moms have a healthy pregnancy, advocate for themselves and know exactly what to expect so they can ease into their new mom identity with confidence and joy.

I help unfulfilled married couples achieve a healthy connection so they can create an environment where they feel seen, heard, and understood again in order to have a happy marriage.

I help parents of young children communicate more effectively with their children so they can have a harmonious household and finally feel in control again without having to yell.

Let's break it down.

Population:

Who has a problem that you'd like to solve? Get as specific as possible with this person. Is it moms or stay at home moms? Is it women or is it African American women? Is it professionals or young professionals? Is it couples or married couples?

When we are selling high ticket, which I'll get to in the next chapter, it's important to hyper-niche down and be as specific as possible. Try to have at least two identifying factors when it comes to your population. You also want to consider how hard or easy it will be to find them. Ideally, you want to have an easy target. Are they all gathered somewhere already? Social media groups? Influencers they follow? Channels they all watch? It will be much easier to market to your population if they are easier to find instead of searching for them like needles in a haystack.

Problem:

If your business is not, at its core, delivering something people want and are willing to pay for, you are setting yourself up for failure. I see a lot of women trying to sell high ticket coaching programs for small problems they are passionate about, but their passion alone isn't always enough for them to be successful. The problem they are solving needs to be a major life problem people are having. People are always buying their way out of something, not into something. Think about all the problems you have paid to solve in your life. Perhaps you had a breakout and got a facial or realized at the last minute you had no clothes for your trip, so you splurged on a shopping spree. Maybe you realized you didn't know enough about something, so you purchased a few trainings on it. Those are just small examples to get you to understand that you have probably bought your way out of a problem before, but I'm sure your biggest investments have come from wanting to see results in your bank account, body, or relationship which goes back to the three biggest markets.

It was the problem and need that led you to purchase and it will be your clients' problems that lead them to you. Luckily, as humans, we tend to have a lot of problems so you Therapreneurs™ have a lot to choose from.

When you are used to solving so many different problems, this can be challenging, so I'd suggest making a list of all the problems you like to solve and are good at solving before fully deciding on one. I want it to be something you are passionate about. Maybe you can even notice a common theme in the problems you are already solving.

Ask yourself these questions:

- Is it costing them? Costing them time, energy, money, confidence, relationships, is it impacting their life in some negative way?

- Will they urgently and eagerly pay you for this? Do they NEED this solved or would it just be a *nice to have?*

- Do they have the funds to pay high ticket prices? This doesn't mean they have to be rich. People will get resourceful, trust me.

- Do they have the time to put in the work to get them from A to B?

- Do you have a warm network already? If so, maybe start there instead of completely picking something different.

- Do they want to avoid something in order to get this result? If so, you can add the word "without" to your niche statement.

- For example, they want to lose weight without sacrificing the foods they love or maybe they want to reduce anxiety without having to take medication.

Solution/Big Outcome:

It's probably the opposite of their problem but, take it a step further and ask yourself what that will do for them. How will it change their life? What is the big outcome?

If you were helping a single mom finally sleep at night, you would want to take it a step further and speak to the fact that she could then be energized and present with her child. This is the big outcome.

If you were helping a single woman feel confident in the dating world, you would want to take it a step further and speak to the fact that she could then find her lifelong partner. This is the big outcome.

Just ask yourself the, "so that ____" question:

- I help (population) achieve/solve (result/problem) so that (biggest benefit, desired outcome-life changing result-big goal).

Making sure your outcome is measurable and visible is key. Remember, no platitudes. The outcome can't just be happiness. If you land on a feeling, you need to take it a step further and ask how this feeling actually shows up in their everyday life. It needs to be real external change and visible. Are they spending more quality time with their kids because they are energized? Are they finally able to stand up in the workplace because they are confident? Are they finally sleeping at night?

I know that your program itself will lead them through the intangibles like the emotional, spiritual, or physical work that you know is required to get your clients lasting results, but we must speak to the tangibles.

It's like giving a dog medicine. They don't want the pill; they want the peanut butter. Sell them peanut butter and give them the pill. Sell them on the tangible and give them the intangible.

And don't get all scared that you can't deliver this big outcome because I know you can. Anyone who has successfully sold a high-ticket program will tell you they went through this fear of not being able to deliver results to their clients. This thought is only normal, and you will never make a promise you can't deliver on. Let service be your motivator. We will talk about imposter syndrome in a future chapter.

Getting to Know Your Client's Pains and Desires

Here is a fun exercise. I want you to pretend you are a fly on the wall in a coffee shop where your ideal client is talking to a friend. First, I want you to list out details and basic demographics. Think about age, gender, marital status, children, passions, personality type, interests, and emotional state. It helps to get a visual in your head. We truly want to know our ideal client better than they know themselves. We have to get on their level in order to speak to them and connect with them emotionally.

Next, I want you to listen to your client talking to their friend. What are their pains? What are their desires? What is the exact language they are using? What is showing up in their life because of their pain? Have they wasted time or missed opportunities because of this pain? If they don't fix this problem right now, what future problems will this cause for them? If they could wave a magic wand and have a dream come true, what would it be? If it's a feeling, then what would that feeling do for them?

Think relationships, finances, confidence, and health. Try to be as specific as possible. If you were your own ideal client, take yourself back and ask your old self these questions too.

Online threads like Reddit can be a powerful tool for finding potential coaching clients and understanding their pains and desires on a much deeper level. Online communities offer a wide variety of forums dedicated to specific topics and interests. Begin by searching for topics related to your niche or area of expertise. Then you can read discussions and participate to offer helpful insight and advice. Be sure to avoid overtly promoting your coaching services as this can come off as spammy. Build rapport and offer free resources first. This can help establish trust with potential clients.

If you know your clients' pains and desires on a deep level you should be able to fill out this sentence!

With my help, my client's life is going to be amazing because _____, but without my help their life is going to continue to be a living hell because _____.

Market Research

By this point you should know who your ideal client is, what burning problems they have, and what big outcome you will get them to. If you don't, the best thing you can do is ask questions. Start by being curious. Get on social media and start asking some market research questions. It doesn't have to be complicated. People love to talk about themselves so typically, it's not that hard to get a few people to answer your questions. Try to speak to as many people as you possibly can to understand what they want and need. Be so curious that you are open to discovering a business idea beyond what you are already imagining.

Market research isn't something you should only do when starting a business. In my opinion, market research never ends. The market is always changing so continuously getting a pulse check and staying connected to changes in the industry will be important for your business, especially if you want to keep happy clients and deliver to them what they need and want. Incentivizing people to engage can be helpful. Maybe you give them a free 15-minute coaching session or token in exchange for their time. Better yet, you can give them a percentage off your coaching program when you release it. After all, it should be your ideal client who you are talking to, right?

Market research can be conducted in many ways. You can ask friends, family, or strangers in online forums if they know anyone who would fit your persona so you could schedule an interview. You could create a poll or survey and send it out. Thanks to the Internet, you can also use existing research. It's possible that someone already conducted research on your industry and target market. Check out Google Scholar before conducting your research.

Here are some questions you can ask people who may be your potential clients:

- What is the single biggest challenge you are having in regard to _____?

- What is the biggest result you want to see right now in this area of your life?

- What ways have you already tried to solve this problem?

- How much time/money have you spent trying to solve this?

- What hasn't worked?

- What are you scared about moving forward toward this goal?

- What would make you doubt you could get those results?

- What way would you like to achieve this result?

- What would be a dream come true as it relates to finding a solution to this problem?

You are Not Looking for Everyone

If you try to be everything for everyone, you will be nothing for no one. That sounds mean but hear me out.

Imagine you had a close friend who was looking for grief support because one of their parents just passed. Who would you send them to? The general therapist/coach who works with clients of any age, race, gender, and issues? Or the specialist who works specifically with parental grief?

Although the modalities and processes you have in place could probably work for everyone, if you try to reach everyone, then you will be spreading yourself too thin and falling on deaf ears. You and your message will be diluted and that is not good because I know you have a bomb message. Just like my poem from earlier, you'll be a four-leaf clover in a massive field. No one will find you and you won't be able to share your gold to transform the lives I know you're meant to.

Just because you focus on a specific target to start doesn't mean that your business has to focus on that audience for forever. Matthew McConaughey went from being known for romantic comedies to being the star in dramas. Will smith went from comedy, to action, to drama, and he even had a rapping career. Oprah Winfrey went from being fired from a news anchor job to a media executive, actress, producer, and billionaire. You can be whoever you want to be at any given moment. Decide who you want to be right now and know that if, and when, you decide to expand, you can.

The idea is to validate your offer with ONE community first then consider expanding your reach. It's in focusing on a specific market that you end up reaching the world. Super counterintuitive, I know! Author and entrepreneur Seth Godin calls this your minimum viable audience. He says, stake out the smallest market you can imagine. The smallest market that can sustain you, the smallest market you can adequately serve. This goes against everything you learned in capitalism school, but in fact, it's the simplest way to matter. (Godin, 2017)

When I came across this concept, it really hit home for me. When I first started my private practice, I didn't quite know who my people were. Yet, I remember going to networking meetings where I had about 60 seconds to say who I was, who I helped, and how I helped, and it was scary as hell. I felt like everyone had their elevator pitch so nailed down and all I had to say was "I'm a licensed clinical social worker and I help anyone and everyone who needs help." My intention was to increase my referrals but in reality, no one understood who they were supposed to refer to me.

As always, when something doesn't work, we pivot. I decided to get super specific with who I helped and how. This was also in the midst of my massive realization that I was actually a coach and not a therapist. So, at my next meeting I said something like this, "Hi, I'm Carly and I'm a women empowerment coach helping millennial women ease through life transitions so they can feel confident in their new identity and life." Although it wasn't perfect, the change made a huge difference. Suddenly, people were coming up to me wanting to know more. They actually had some context to grab from. I figured I would get even more specific at the next meeting, and I said, "Hi, I'm Carly and I'm a spiritual empowerment coach who helps millennial women going through a major life transformational experience with ease and confidence in their new identity all through the power of energy healing." I had people asking me if I helped women who were moving, going through a divorce, getting married, or changing careers? The answer was, yes! All of a sudden, I was getting a ton of referrals for my soulmate clients.

All that time I had feared narrowing myself down because it felt limiting, but it was quite the opposite. I realized I didn't have to be for everyone. The funny part is I still go to these meetings, and now I present myself as "Hi, I'm Carly and I'm a business coach for psychotherapists and I help them build highly profitable online coaching businesses." Talk about a 360-niche change.

Again, you can be whoever you want to be at any given time. But whoever you choose to be...be it with all your might! Don't half-ass your identity just because it feels uncomfortable stepping into it. Claim it, own it, and shout it to the rooftops!

The idea is to start small and grow big. I started with psychotherapists and now I work with all sorts of licensed clinicians, such as occupational therapists and speech therapists. I have even helped friends in the film, fitness, and real estate industry build their online courses too. Start small, grow big.

We are always growing and learning, and we are ever evolving. I know it can be scary to make these big decisions sometimes because with our decisions comes an identity shift, but I want to give you permission to be a new person anytime you choose. I give you permission to change your niche at any time you choose. Nothing is permanent. However, with that being said, I think it's important to stay with a niche long enough to experience trial and error. If you niche hop repeatedly solely because your target isn't responding, you may need to look at other pieces of the puzzle such as your messaging, positioning, and offer before making the leap. I suggest being 80% sure about your niche and committing. I also suggest making sure all those other pieces of the puzzle are in check too, which I will get into later.

Now that you have an overview of who you help and how you help, you can begin outlining your course. It's a lot simpler than you might think. Consider the problem your ideal client has and the solution you are getting them too and ask yourself what are the six to eight milestones they have to go through in order to get there? These six to eight milestones become the modules for your course.

For our clients, it's:

1. Knowing the difference between therapy and coaching and protecting your license

2. Deciding your niche

3. Mapping out your signature program

4. Marketing your signature program

5. Selling your signature program

6. Delivering your signature program

7. Creating a strong brand

8. Having a do or die badass mindset

Once it's mapped out, you can begin creating trainings under each module. Essentially, it's a curriculum to get your client from problem to solution. I recommend creating PowerPoint slides and then a video or audio of you teaching the slides. Then you'll upload that to a course hosting platform service so you can give your clients access when they enroll.

This is how you leverage your time. You could be relaxing on the beach while your clients are watching your training videos. You will want to have at least one to two group coaching calls a week to answer your clients' questions, provide support, and hold them accountable.

Recap:

If you don't articulate the power of what you do, who you do it with, and how you specifically help, you will be the world's best kept secret.

Understand your client's pain and desires so you can connect with them emotionally and intimately and motivate them to take action right now. Ask yourself, what are the six to eight milestones my client has to go through right now to get to the solution?

Step into your new identity and own it.

PS: If you are ready to step into your coaching identity NOW visit www.carlyhillcoaching.com to book your no cost strategy session so we can discuss the exact steps you need to take to become a successful online coach!

Chapter 3

The Business Model

Understand my secret formula for pricing your program high ticket and how you can be paid to create an asset in your business that will help you reduce your hours. Get proof that you are the Beyonce of your space and stand out as the expert in the saturated coaching market!

She pulled over in her car to take my call, dug out her notepad and said, "I'm ready, and I've been looking forward to this call all week." Kelsey was ready to hear all I had to say about this so-called model that could help her triple her therapy income. I could hear the eagerness in her voice to finally have the freedom and flexibility she craved as a busy mom. I also felt the energetic skepticism of, is this too good to be true?

She said, "I can't keep living like this. I love what I do but I'm burning the wick at all ends." Kelsey was seeing back-to-back clients in her private practice to make ends meet for her family and pay back her student loans. She loved the work she was doing with clients, but she didn't love the admin work, inconsistent caseload due to turnover and seasonality, and lack of time she had with her family. She wanted something different, but not totally. All she really wanted was to be able to help people while simultaneously living a balanced life.

I've met with countless Kelsey's before. They usually come to me in one of two ways. They are either exhausted and overextended from doing the one-on-one work, not making enough money, and not having any time left in the day or they are proactive and can see that what they are doing right now will not be sustainable in the long run and they need to make a change before it's too late.

Within three months, my team and I showed them how to create their business entity, protect their license, create ONE signature group coaching program within their expertise, market it on social media, and sell it at a high-ticket price. It's the A to Z.

The key point to creating a group program within your niche is to leverage your time and get paid for your knowledge. The days of seeing one-on-one clients and only getting paid when your butt is in the therapy chair is old news. New news is tapping into the one-to-many model, packaging and recording your expertise, and hopping on one to two group coaching calls a week to answer questions about what your clients are learning in the course.

The days of only helping people within your state is old news too. As long as you are not treating the client for medical necessity, you can help clients nationwide and globally with your expertise. This is the beauty of the online world. The rise of the digital economy is here to stay, and it's been growing exponentially. If there is anything 2020 showed us, it's that online education is our future. The coaching industry is a 20-billion-dollar industry. According to Global Market Insights the eLearning projection is one trillion USD by 2028. (Wadhwan & Gankar, 2022)

If you have something of value to teach, now is the time to tap into online education. The market is only going to get more saturated. It's not too late for you. It's saturated because there is a need. Just because a market is crowded doesn't mean you can't succeed. The biggest determinant of your success is not the market, but YOU. Your time to dominate is now. These are goldmine times.

You Only Need ONE

When we analyze our time allocation, it's easy to see focusing on ONE offer is key to success. Every single woman who can teach something of value can package their expertise into a high-ticket program and hop on two group coaching calls a week.

A lot of women don't start their coaching business or disregard the thought of creating an online course because they think they will be stuck building content for the rest of their lives. They think they have to create a new course every month or so and create new social media content every day for God knows how long. The thought of this gives me a headache too and it sounds horrible. It's the exact opposite of what I teach.

Many women follow this model thinking creating MORE will help them reach their goals. We live in a society that teaches us that more is better. Someone once told me that the magic is in the subtraction and not the addition. I wish I could remember who told me that because it changed my life and it's so true. At the time of hearing that, I was in the more mentality. Chasing after every single idea that popped into my head, spreading myself thin, and left without a sustainable profit in the end.

It's common. Women in the more mentality go off and create courses in ALL their areas of expertise. To them, it seems like they are doing the right thing. They have something for everyone, and constant creation feeds their ambitious entrepreneurial soul. In theory, it seems good but, it's the perfect recipe for burnout. It looks like hustling with no reward. Plus, it creates confusion and overwhelm for the buyer. There are too many choices! Your coaching service suite should not be comparable to a Chinese restaurant menu.

Constantly re-launching with a new course is very overwhelming for newbie course creators, not to mention it's exhausting and annoying, but it's the only way they can think of in order to hit their revenue goals. It typically looks like hours upon hours creating, marketing, and enrolling just to break even. The worst part is, if she wanted and needed 10 women to hit her goals but only got three, then she still has to deliver the full program exhausted. Unexcitingly delivering a program with a negative profit margin is not in my vocabulary and neither is creating a course and hoping and praying your current audience in your current course will buy into it. This is not a sustainable business model, it's madness.

What is sustainable you might ask?

Having ONE signature coaching program and focusing all your energy on just this ONE and doing it really well. This is the magic of subtraction. Perhaps down the road you have a graduate problem, backend offer, or a mini course but this should only be added once your ONE signature program is up and running like a well-oiled machine. There is an order of operations that should be followed.

I'm also a firm believer in open/rolling enrollment, meaning clients can come into the program at any time. This is going to save you a ton of "launch" headache. This means that if you have a three-month program then you would have a person in month two in your program on a coaching call as well as a person in week two. Person in month two is going to ask much more powerful questions than person in week two, and the person in week two will probably bring month two person back to the basics. This is the beauty of osmosis learning. It's proven to be the most effective way to help your clients see what is not in their experience. They are going to grow mentally, spiritually, and emotionally and maybe even financially and physically too, just by being around others on a similar path. Everyone loves the opportunity to connect with other individuals who share similar aspirations and challenges. It creates a unique sense of shared purpose and accountability.

It's one of the best things you can do in your business. It helps you leverage your time while simultaneously getting your clients faster results. Plus, it's much easier to not show up for yourself when no one sees you. Have you ever had a one-on-one client fade off? It's easy for them because no one else is watching versus being seen and known in a group environment. It's not just about them anymore; it's about a community. They may have felt supported by one of the other members and they know they need to show up to keep supporting the others. It's the sense of belonging that will sustain the momentum to help someone continue moving forward and overcome obstacles.

This model of open enrollment and group coaching works so well because the recorded course is in place. Most of the teaching is done in the recorded course and the coaching and questions are addressed on the support calls.

If you were to choose to do cohort, also known as open close, open close every three months or however long your program is, then you would be doing a lot of work preparing for launches and you might miss people because you'd have a waitlist. The impulse might not be there for the client when you finally open again.

With open enrollment, there are plenty of ways you can creatively re-package and promote your ONE offer over and over again to keep it fresh and appealing for your potential clients.

She was Sitting on a Gold Mine

Let's talk numbers for a second. I've always hated math, but these math problems are incredibly fun and relevant.

Understanding the true value of high ticket is key to unlocking your financial dreams. Selling high ticket is how you transform your own life while simultaneously transforming others' lives through your signature high ticket program. It's a win-win. High ticket is the best ticket and low ticket, or trading dollars for hours, is old news.

You may be wondering what high ticket means. High ticket usually starts at $2,000 and sky is the limit. I've seen plenty of coaching programs and courses that go for $15,000-$50,000 and even higher. Low ticket is usually $500 or less.

Let's start with your revenue goal. The vast majority of online coaches make less than six figures a year. While you may be very comfortable generating $8-10k months, and that is where you'll most likely start, I'd like to future pace you to bigger and better revenue goals to show you what is possible.

Let's start with your revenue goal of $500k. I know half a million a year might seem crazy to you right now but stick with me. We like to dream big around here. Five-hundred thousand a year means you need to be making roughly $40k a month.

Reaching $40k a month with back-to-back one-on-one sessions is nearly impossible unless you are charging high prices. Regardless, you'd still be trading dollars for hours. The average going rate for one-on-one sessions is $150 per session. So, if you saw eight one-on-one sessions five days a week at $150, you'd still only be at $24k a month. I'd imagine you would be extremely exhausted. Perhaps this is already a life you're living. If so, I hope it's not for long.

How about if you decided to package your knowledge into a course instead to leverage your time and you decided to price it at $497. Sounds fair?

Now, how many new people do you think you need to sell your course to in order to make $40k months with your $497 course?

It's 80. Eight zero. Insert scared face.

Selling 80 people your course EVERY SINGLE MONTH is incredibly hard. You would have to have a massive following to do this successfully. Studies show that the standard conversion rate is 3% which would mean you would have to get your offer in front of almost 3,000 people. Even if you have 3,000 followers on Instagram™, or in a Facebook™ group, doesn't mean that all of them will see your offer. Usually, only hundreds would see it and then only 3% of those hundreds would convert. Again, this model works for people with really big followings but not for the masses.

Now, how about you decide to package your expertise into a high end, high touch, transformational and supportive program and sell it at 5k instead.

How many new clients a month do you think you need to hit half a million a year?

You would need eight. That is two new clients per week. That is it! You think you can handle getting two new clients a week? I do! Especially when you are following a proven lead generation strategy to call in these perfect fit clients.

These are the numbers that make sense and I want you to dream even bigger and double this. If you can get 16 new clients per month you could be a millionaire in one year.

Who Would Pay for This?

At this point, you're probably like, okay Carly, this sounds great but who the hell is going to pay me $5,000 for my signature coaching program when people already expect me to be free or covered by their co-pay?

Let me tell you a quick story.

There was once a flea in a jar experiment where researchers placed fleas in a jar with no lid and they jumped out. They then placed the fleas in a jar with a lid, so the fleas jumped and hit the lid over and over. But then the researchers removed the lid and guess what happened? The fleas jumped only as high as if the lid was still on. They were conditioned by an invisible ceiling.

I want you to ask yourself if there is an invisible ceiling right now on your income?

Now, therapists, I am not trying to compare you to a flea, but I do want you to think about this question. Are you putting an invisible ceiling on how much you charge? Perhaps the price you charge for one-on-one sessions was created out of thin air with no math involved so that you could just hope and pray your dream lifestyle would pan out?

Perhaps now that I'm speaking about you selling your high-ticket program at 5k it is bringing up all sorts of feelings. You might be worrying that people will say no to you and that is bringing up self-doubt or maybe you feel like you aren't qualified enough which can bring up shame and guilt. More commonly, the fear of failure always seems to creep in which can lead to anxiety and a lack of self-confidence.

Whatever it is, just know that it is normal.

Hear me out!

Your fee has nothing to do with what you think you are worth. You are quite literally transforming someone's life. No one can put a price tag on that. However, you are putting a price tag on it because you have a life to live.

It has nothing to do with your experience or how many certifications you have. Stop comparing yourself. You do good work, you know it, own it.

It has nothing to do with how long you've been a therapist. Studies actually show that the longer you're in the field the worse you get. I laughed when I heard that too but yes, we must stay up with the times.

It has nothing to do with giving back. You can do that in other ways when you can actually afford it. You come first.

If you'd like to calculate what your exact rate in private practice should be do the math here https://feecalculator.carlyhillcoaching.com/

I am going to digress from my money pep talk because what's really important to focus on first is the difference between a program and a course.

To me, a course is a recorded course alone, also known as evergreen. This means it lives on forever. There is no additional support or coaching. It's do-it-yourself and the client is responsible for doing everything on their own.

Then, you have a program. This consists of added support one way or another. You will have DFY (done for you) or DWY (done with you) or maybe a combination of both.

The top 1% of coaches are using the hybrid model of an evergreen course and added support/coaching and selling it at a high-ticket price. This is what I teach. So, when you hear me refer to your signature coaching program, this is what I mean: one recorded course, group coaching calls, and added support in between the coaching calls.

So back to the question, Carly, how am I going to get a high-ticket client into my hybrid signature coaching program?

The answer is easy. There are seven billion people in this world. There is no shortage of people who are waking up every morning investing high ticket dollars in coaching. There is certainly no shortage of people who need help. The reality is people are waiting and wishing for you. There is someone who is praying for you and your help right now. However, there is absolutely an art and a science to creating a high-ticket offer that people will pay for.

First off, people value what they pay premium prices for. If your clients invest in themselves at a high-ticket price, then they are going to take their transformation seriously. When people pay, they pay attention. They are the A+ students who do their homework, show up to the calls, and expect to reach their outcome.

Believe it or not, it actually feels good for them to invest in a high-end transformation because they know they are going to get the result. It's worth it to them. Even when people choose to work with you one-on-one, they are paying for their transformation, not calls with you. People don't invest in coaches for Zoom calls or video training. They invest for a transformation and that feels good to them. It's like buying a first-class airplane ticket. If someone buys first-class, they do so knowing that they are going to get top-notch treatment and feel rested when they arrive. It felt good for them to upgrade.

It's the same thing with your high-ticket coaching program. It's worth it for them to hire you to get the results faster, easier, and with a proven system. The key is, they know they will get their results. This is why they are investing thousands to work with you. It's really the accountability, support, and expertise they are buying when they invest in your program.

It doesn't feel as good to buy a low-ticket course. I can't tell you the number of times I've personally bought a low-ticket course, and it's just sat there on my computer. It was a "nice to have," it wasn't a necessity, so I didn't show up for it the way I did when I invested thousands of dollars for a major need of mine. People have also become weary of online courses these days because there are so many of them. They shop around, compare prices, and buy the most appealing and least expensive, unoriginal, and mildly transformational one.

Usually, these low-ticket courses are ones that are a hot commodity. For example, someone may purchase a course on how to do reels or create a podcast. These are courses that are available at multiple places and probably consist of mostly the same content. This means that they will most likely go with the cheapest one. You do not want to be in this category. Instead, you want to be in your own separate category where they can't even put a price tag on the value that you are providing. Your program is based on value, not price. They can't shop around for programs like yours because your program is a category of one, best in class program, and you're the Beyoncé of this space. More will come on this topic later.

Let's pretend your potential client, Sally, has three choices.

Sally is a single mom of three who can't fall asleep at night. It's impacting her energy levels and productivity in her career and as a mom. She is feeling mom guilt for raising her kids without another parent, for slacking in her career, and for not feeling as energized and present when she is with the kids. Her stress is reaching new levels and she is looking for an immediate solution.

She could:

- Take a recorded do-it-yourself, one size fits all recorded course to help her fall asleep for $197

- Go to therapy for three years, even though she isn't meeting medical necessity, for $150 a session and spend $36k

- Come into your high-end, high-touch, transformational, and supportive three-month coaching program, where you specifically work with moms exactly like her for $5k

What do you think she would rather do?

Most likely, she ruled out number one knowing that it probably wouldn't provide the lasting result she needed or maybe she's already tried that option. She then decided to save two years and nine months of her life, and $31k, and go with option number three, your signature coaching program.

It's a win-win. Not only does this serve you better as a business owner but it serves Sally better to get a faster result. You are helping her skip steps, hold her accountable, and avoid any mistakes that may prolong her transformation.

Now what about if Sally wanted to learn how to meal prep healthy meals for her kids? This is something that has been on her mind, but it would be a "nice to have," it's not a burning need like sleep. Plus, this would be a one size fits all do-it-yourself course where she could download easy meal prep recipes and watch videos on how to prep. Sleep will transform Sally's life. Learning to meal prep will not. A sleep program can be sold at a high-ticket price. A meal prep course wouldn't be successful at the same price. My point here is don't just create a program for anything you're "good at" and can teach. It has to solve a major problem.

Create Your High Ticket Offer

Creating an offer that is valued at five to ten times more than what your client is paying is a good rule of thumb. So, if your program cost $1,000 then its real-world value would be at least $5,000. The idea is that the perceived value of your program is so high, your potential clients can understand and see that. This way, they don't get sticker shock when you tell them the investment. The reason people buy anything is because they feel like they are getting a deal. Everyone loves a bargain. Have you ever bought something completely irrelevant that you didn't need just because you couldn't pass up the deal, so you somehow justified it in your head and just got it? Maybe you like to shop the clearance aisles for this reason because it feels good to get a deal. If so, you probably firmly believed what you were getting (the value) was worth way more than what you paid (the price).

The $31k Sally would save (perceived value) makes it a no-brainer decision for her to come into your coaching program versus three years of therapy. Sometimes, the value cannot be quantified numerically and that's okay. You can do a fun math problem to make it quantifiable. What would it be worth for Sally to finally be able to sleep at night, excel in her career, and be energized and present in the home with her kids? Probably priceless! She is dying for this, right?

Well, if you asked her if it would be worth $10 a day, she'd probably say yes and if you were to multiply that by three years then technically she is telling you that in order to finally be able to sleep at night, excel in her career, and be energized and present in the home for the next three years it would be worth $10,950 and probably much more because she wouldn't only want that for the next three years. Your program is going to teach her how to achieve all of this in three months for less than half that price and the skills she learns will stay with her for a lifetime.

Would Sally think it's worth it? I'd sure hope so.

I don't teach my clients to start selling their coaching programs at $5,000. The first time they sell their program, it should be significantly discounted. I recommend 50% for the first go around. This is their beta round or founding members round. In the online coaching and consulting world, we call this proof of concept. Every large company has beta programs, like Apple or

Tesla. This is because proof of concept is critical and should be established before dedicating time and money into mass marketing.

I don't teach my clients to start selling their coaching program at $500 either. Pricing is never permanent but it's really hard to increase your price from $500 to $5,000. If you are offering your first few clients your $5,000 program for $2,500-$3,500 and it will never be that price again, you are at least in the same ballpark, and it's incentivizing your clients to get it now, while they can, to get the deal.

This scares a lot of women. They always want their clients to be happy and they are afraid that they will charge too much, and their client will not be satisfied with their result. Charging too much or too little is subjective. You should not charge more than your offer is worth, but you should charge far more than it cost you to deliver or fulfill it. This is how you will scale.

Companies like Gucci, Louis Vuitton, and Prada are known for charging exorbitant prices for their designer clothing and accessories. The cost of producing these items is often a small fraction of the retail price, but the brands command high prices due to their exclusivity, craftsmanship, and branding. The same goes for pharmaceutical companies, technology companies, and even coffee shops like Starbucks.

You Can't Control Other People's Outcomes

The fact of the matter is you can't control other people's outcomes. Many clients won't do all of the work when and how they are supposed to, based on what you're teaching, and that is not your fault. You can't do their work. Your job is to deliver everything you know to deliver in order to get the client results, just like you have with others.

The goal here is to work with clients as soon as possible. In order to build momentum, you need to work with a small set of clients and solve their specific problem. Three to five clients are perfect for your beta round. Not only will this get you out of your head and into service but it will also help you get feedback so you can make your program the best of the best. Your beta clients will give you feedback in exchange for the value you are providing. Getting feedback is one of the best gifts you can receive. As a business owner, you always want to strive for improvement. Scheduling check in sessions or feedback surveys will be crucial to ensuring your clients are getting the most out of your offerings.

Get Paid to Deliver Your Beta

Yes, you read that right. You can get paid to create an asset in your business that will help you reduce your hours by 80%. In fact, I would strongly advise you not to do it any other way. Most business coaches will agree with me on this one. You must sell before you create. You do not want to spend weeks and weeks creating your course and curriculum and then go to market and sell it. I have seen too many people do this and it flopped. What a waste of time!

Instead, you just want to create the outline of your program and your offer stack, which I will explain further on. I know it seems crazy to sell something you haven't yet created but it doesn't mean you aren't in integrity. You know exactly what you are offering. Maybe you've even started to build out the beginning to create a runway for your clients or to drip them the content as they go. They will be watching week one while you create week two, and so on and so forth.

Be the Beyoncé of Your Space

Many coaches and healers just starting out have a big fear that the market for their services is so crowded that they won't possibly be able to stand out. Let me ask you this, is there any shortage of people who need help?

To attract clients, especially in a crowded market, you need to know the value you offer, what makes you unique, and why someone should buy from you. Introspection is key. Then, you need to let your audience know.

In the book The Blue Ocean Strategy, they call a saturated market a "red ocean," a market that is so busy that all the "big fish" are already established and if you joined the fight and tried to compete as a "small fish" you would get eaten alive. (Kim & Mauborgne, 2015) It echoes the old proverb that you should fish where the fish are plenty, but the fishermen are few.

Cirque du Soleil is a perfect example of a blue ocean strategy. Circuses in the 1980s were dominated by Ringling Bros. and Barnum & Bailey. They featured three-ring circuses, clowns, and animal acts, and their customers were children and families. The competition was really strong.

However, a former street performer, Guy Laliberté decided to escape the red ocean of circuses to create a blue ocean of theatrical entertainment, Cirque du Soleil. Its shows combine the circus with adult theater, showing incredible acrobatics and physical feats set to a storyline and original music. Freaking genius!

Cirque du Soleil distinguished itself and became a category of one or as I like to call it, the Beyoncé of its space. Cirque du Soleil's goal wasn't to outperform the competition or be the best in the industry. Instead, it was to operate within that new space, making the competition immaterial.

In order to create your own blue ocean brand or business means you need to find an intersection between your passions and your expertise. Being an expert in your space is a lot easier than it sounds. It doesn't mean you have to be the absolute best in the world. A wise man knows he knows nothing, but it does require that you've done something over and over again until you've become really good at it, if not better than most.

To be successful in the coaching space, you need to be known for something and you need to stand out. You also need to be real and transparent. Real people love real people. Don't be afraid to peel back the layers and be vulnerable.

What Makes You Special

If I could take a guess, I'd bet that you have had some experiences in your life that you have learned from that could somehow impact a stranger's life. You've probably learned a lesson or two about health, wealth, relationships, or life in general, right? Maybe you had a big turning point? A difficult situation that you now look back on with gratitude seeing that it happened for a reason. All of these experiences play an important role in your business and they will become part of your brand story. I'd encourage you to do some journaling on this.

The next thing to think about is your expertise. You might have already done a bit of thinking on this in the previous chapter, but I really want you to have a hard think about your expertise right now.

Try asking yourself these questions:

- What topics do you have extensive knowledge on? The topic that you could ramble on about for hours.

- What could you confidently teach someone else to do or about?

- What questions do people ask you about often?

- What skills have you developed over time?

- If you asked other people what you were good at, what would they say?

Lastly, I want you to think about your natural born gifts.

There could be 100's of people doing similar coaching to you, but no one can do it the way YOU do it. There is only ONE you. You are special. The truth is people need you because you are you. You are the only person who has your experience, your story, your wisdom, your unique genius. Again, in case no one has told you recently, you are special.

Every time I sit at an airport bar, I always end up knowing a complete stranger's life story. And not just surface level stuff. I remember one man in particular in the Las Vegas airport. I was so hungover from a weekend trip with my girls, but the bar was the only place I could find a spot to order my pizza, so I plopped myself down and sure enough before you know it the man next to me was telling me his deepest darkest relationship secrets that he said he has only told one other person before. I'm not sure how I stuck it out for that one with my partly cloudy brain, but I did.

For whatever reason, everywhere I go, it's like I have a sticky note on my forehead that says talk to me and share what's on your mind. It's not like these people know I'm a therapist and I wouldn't dare tell them because who knows how much more they would open up if I did. I never really mind; it's just an interesting observation I have made.

I've also always been the go-to friend when someone needs to process something, vent, or share a secret. I think people just feel comfortable around me. I've always been told, "Your energy is so calming" and "I feel like you won't judge me."

I'm sure social work school elevated this but for as long as I can remember, I've always been this way. I consider it one of my superpowers. It's a natural born gift of mine to make people feel comfortable enough to vulnerably share what's on their mind, sometimes without me even saying a word. This is something that helps me in my business every day.

I'd encourage you to reflect on your very own superpowers so that you can see how you can bring those superpowers into your business and how they make you stand out from your competition. What do people often say about you? What do people usually come to you for? What things come easily to you?

Sometimes what you decide to coach on seems completely out of left field but it's something you have a passion for. Maybe you'll combine a passion of yours with your background in the helping field?

For example, Jenna came to me saying she wanted to help stressed out women. Now, we know that was not specific enough, but it was a good start. When she started to tell me about her passions and interests and told me she loved acting, I went on to ask her if she ever thought about helping actresses excel in their career and push past the stress that comes along with auditions and her face LIT UP. It wasn't even something that had crossed her mind prior because it seemed so separate.

Another one of my clients wanted to do women empowerment coaching targeting women who were going through transitions, but she actually ended up teaching real estate agents how to transition into the next level position due to her passion and expertise in the industry and she was able to combine her love for mental health into her program.

Nothing is off the table. The only box you're ever in is the one you put around yourself.

Write Your Brand Story

One of the best ways to stand out in the saturated market and connect with your ideal client is to tell them your story, especially if you were your own ideal client. Your story will sell. Share your journey of struggles and success so your clients can connect with you on a deeper level.

Writing your brand story also gives you a chance to showcase your personality. Your tone, writing style, and personal anecdotes can communicate your approach and philosophy, which can be attractive to potential clients. No one has the same stories you do. No one can do what you do or how you do it. Everyone resonates with different energies.

Lastly, writing your story builds credibility. It can help you establish yourself as an authority in your field. By sharing your qualifications, experiences, and successes, you can demonstrate your expertise and build trust with potential clients.

Creating Your Offer

By now, you should know who you help, how you help them, and what makes you different as a coach. You should also have an idea of how you would like to price your offer and how many beta clients that discounted price will stand for. If you don't, that is okay. Take your time. It's the foundation of your business so it's incredibly important. If you do know then you are ready to move on and create your high-ticket offer.

The first thing you want to do is to give your offer a name. A clear and concise name. This is key. You don't want a cutesy name or a name that will confuse people. You need a name that will speak to the population you are serving and the outcome you are providing. If it happens to rhyme, cool but don't get caught up on it. You can always change the name down the road; you aren't trademarking anything right away. Google or AI (Artificial Intelligence) might be your best friend as you brainstorm. You can also check out a phrase generator or a thesaurus. Make a list of keywords your ideal client would resonate with then start to move pieces around like a puzzle until you have a name that you like. Don't spend too much time on this.

The next part of designing your offer is creating your stack. This is your real offer. It's all the deliverables inside your signature coaching program. Your stack will most likely grow and change over time so don't sweat trying to make your offer as grandiose as some of the more established coaches you've probably seen floating around social media. Creating your stack should only take you a week or so. Don't overcomplicate it. The beautiful thing about it is, you create it once and you get to repeat it often to multiple different potential clients. It's high leverage work.

In order to create your stack (all the value you are offering) I want you to pull out the list of problems your client is having. You should have jotted these down already. Then I want you to reverse engineer the problem by asking yourself "what do I need to teach them or do for them in order to solve this?" Put it into solution-oriented language. All of the solutions will become your offer stack.

Example:

Problem: Communication Issues with Partner

- Learn the power of healthy communication following

my cordial communication scripts that I use to help my clients quickly form a healthy connection with their partner again.

Problem: Lacking intimacy

- How to increase your intimacy so you can feel hot and steamy with your sex life.

Problem: Fighting all the time

- How to handle conflict with ease so every situation doesn't turn into an argument.

Bonus: Workshop from somatic energy healer to clear energetic blocks that could be holding you back from deep dream connection you strive to have with your partner.

Guarantee: Seven-day money back if you feel the relationship roadmap program isn't right for you.

Make sure you include bonuses and a guarantee. Bonuses help you increase your perceived value, and a guarantee helps you lower the risk for your client. You want your client to think, "Holy cow, I get all of this for only this price? And there is no downside to me taking this leap. I'm in!" It would be a no-brainer, bomb offer.

While your offer should be of high value to your clients, it should cost you less to deliver it. Your goal is to have the highest profit margin possible while also delivering the best experience possible for your clients. You should have a rather large list of solutions that you reverse engineered from the problems your potential clients are having. Take a look at them and remove the solutions that are of high cost and low value, especially for your beta round. I like to call this trimming the fat. Only providing them with what is absolutely necessary in order to get from problem to solution. People don't want fluff, they want results.

Social Proof

It's always okay to over deliver so try to under promise and overdeliver. The first time you ever deliver your program, you should aim to deliver a ton of value. You need great testimonials and social proof in order to keep getting new clients. Happy clients equal a happy business for you. Over delivering will get you great client reviews. Great client reviews provide a level of trust with potential clients that you are a real coach who gets clients real results. People don't want to just hear about your story and how you got yourself results. They want to hear about how you got other people results.

According to CXL experimentation agency, begin with research conducted online before the purchase is made. (Laja, 2022) Just think about the last time you went to purchase something online or went to a new restaurant. Most likely, you probably read the reviews first in order to build trust before making the purchase. Reading reviews has become our new normal in a world full of skeptics. There is no shortage of pop-up coaches and genius marketers out there but coaches who have a genuine following and get their clients amazing results are harder to stumble upon.

When you have amazing reviews and social proof, it will help you stand out in the saturated market. Take screenshots of your client's progress and wins along the way to share it with other potential clients. Encourage them to share these wins. We call this social proof in the coaching world. According to dynamic yield, social proof is a psychological phenomenon where people assume the actions of others in an attempt to reflect correct behavior for a given situation. (*What is social proof?*, 2020) In essence, it's the notion that, since others are doing it, I should be doing it, too.

Schedule check-ins to ensure you are getting constructive feedback throughout the beta round. You will want to listen more and talk less. Hearing feedback from real time clients is one of the best things you can do to improve your program. Right after the beta round is over, I would highly suggest scheduling a time where they can give you a wonderful video testimonial about the great work you did together. In the testimonial video you will want to ask them where they were before they started working with you and what problems they had and where they are now. You will also want to ask them what their big takeaways were and how they are applying that to their life now. Lastly, you will want to address some of their fears or objections they had prior to coming into your program (other potential clients may have these too) and how taking the leap of faith to work with you was well worth it.

Success stories are one of the fastest ways to attract high-quality leads and turn them into paying clients. It's a sales driving shortcut. It shows other people what is truly possible. It's one of your greatest marketing assets, period. According to impact plus, testimonials can increase . (Johnson, 2021) Whether we like it or not, our decisions are always either consciously or subconsciously influenced by the choices, opinions, and actions of the people around us; it's just the way life works. Psychologist Robert Cialdini writes in his bestselling book, "Whether the question is what to do with an empty popcorn box in a movie theater, how fast to drive on a certain stretch of highway, or how to eat the chicken at a dinner party, the actions of those around us will be important in defining the answer." (Cialdini, 2021)

Examples of My Testimonials

Carly gave me tools to help me gain focus and perspective on what's important to me, introduced me to new mindset shifts and ways of thinking about business that were not even on my radar. I use the things I learned with Carly daily.

Working with Carly saved me an enormous amount of time, frustration and lack of momentum in my business building. Not to mention my sanity.

Carly's program and coaching sessions took the utter overwhelm out of the picture and broke everything down into manageable action steps. Oh so helpful, especially when it comes to social media and website content copy - a life saver!

When I first realized I wanted to become a coach, I had no idea what steps to take and Carly was able to help me shift my mindset and believe in my coaching business making me feel capable and empowered. With Carly's step by step program, I was able to create a solid foundation and learn how to build and become successful in my business. My work with Carly was paramount to my journey and I wouldn't be where I am today without our solid and beautiful work together.

I was so impressed by how Carly showed up. She was always prepared and so good at generating ideas. There were some days where I felt so uninspired and stuck (lots of limiting beliefs about myself, feelings of not being 'good enough') and she was able to help me see past them and really start to believe in myself.

I feel so grateful to have found Carly. I thought I was just hiring someone to teach me the ins and outs of creating and marketing my signature coaching offer. And believe me, Carly knows her stuff! But what I got was so much more. She teaches from a conscious and aligned place that inspires me to constantly challenge any fear-based doubts that I have, work on my mindset, expand my vision, and step into my role on this earth as the true agent of change that I am. During our calls, she creates such a comfortable space and is always ready for any question I throw at her. I could not do this without her!

These are only a few!

If you'd like to see more direct client results, please visit https://www.carlyhillcoaching.com/testimonial

Recap:

- Creating a group program within your niche will help you leverage your time!

- You only need ONE offer! Reverse engineer your clients' problems to create it!

- High ticket is the best ticket. Yes, people will pay.

- Get paid to create it for the first time and get those testimonials asap!

- Be the Beyoncé of your space and know what makes you different.

PS: Join the Therapist to Coach Accelerator™ Facebook™ group to get access to FREE trainings on offer creation and standing out in the saturated market!

Chapter 4

Marketing

Implement my Modern Marketing Masterplan client attraction system to organically attract qualified soul mate clients on social media. No more marketing mysteries. I literally give you the step-by-step plan to attract paying clients and get more booked calls on your calendar.

Marketing: the action or business of promoting and selling products or services.

The goal of marketing is to reach your target audience, help them identify if your offer is right for them or not, and invite them to buy your product or service. It's a lot like dating. If you were searching for a partner, you would likely only hang out in places where your ideal partner would. From there, you'd most likely try to do something to get their attention or put yourself in a position where you could be noticed. After that, it would naturally move into a rapport building conversation that would hopefully lead to an exchange of information and or a date.

Think of marketing just like this. You first need to know where your ideal client is hanging out, online or offline. Then you need to be able to get noticed and spark a conversation. This would move them along in the client journey so you can hop on a consultation call with them, tell them about your product or service, and make it easy for them to say yes to buying from you.

Let's break it down.

Find Your Ideal Client

In order for your customer to buy from you, you need to know where your audience is. This is why hyper niching and targeting a subset population is so important. The more specific you are with who you are targeting, the easier it will be for you to market your business.

You don't need to promote yourself everywhere, but you do need to be a walking billboard in the places where your ideal client is hanging out. If you don't know where your ideal client is hanging out, market research will be imperative before you can attract quality leads and maintain a business that is customer driven. You should aim to know your ideal client better than they know themselves. What are they googling? What events do they attend? What Facebook groups are they in? What influencers do they follow? Whose email list are they on? What websites do they frequent? We covered all of this in the previous chapters but it's worth a recap.

Get Noticed

In order to get the date, you must first be noticed. In order to get the sale or consult call, you must first be noticed. After you find your ideal client and get in front of them, you must capture their attention. In a world with so many people and attention spans so short, you must stand out. In the online world, this means you need to be posting compelling content to stop the scroll. Think about your own use of social media. How often are you skimming or scrolling? What gets you to stop and read something? Most likely, it's a compelling first line, also known as the hook. It was probably calling out to something you desire or a big pain point of yours. Keep this in mind when you are creating content and posting for your audience. You must get their attention.

Anytime you have a promotion or sale coming up, you should be telling your audience days or even weeks in advance that you have an exciting announcement coming soon. People love to be amped up and it builds anticipation, excitement and curiosity. I would suggest providing 80% value and promoting your service 20% of the time.

Have a Conversation

Conversions happen because of conversations not because of followers, likes, or getting noticed. Grabbing your ideal client's attention is only the first step in solidifying the sale, or in the dating world, grabbing their attention is only the first step before you actually get the date. A genuine rapport building conversation needs to happen prior to even knowing if a date would be worthwhile. It's the same thing for moving the client along in the journey. How would you know if they would be a good fit for your services if you didn't first ask some probing questions to identify their needs and areas of concern. Some people get choked up when they are having an online messenger conversation because it doesn't feel as natural but, in reality, it's the same conversation you would be having in person if you were face-to-face. Keep this in mind if you ever feel awkward behind the keyboard.

The Exchange

After you have a genuine conversation in the dating world, you would most likely exchange phone numbers. In business, this could mean either getting their business card, email or possibly giving them a piece of valuable content to build the know, like, and trust factor even more. In some cases, you might go straight for the date and invite them to a free consult call with you. In my humble opinion, it's necessary to have a free consultation call with a potential client, especially when you are selling a high-ticket service.

There is usually some type of resistance to exchanging information. Whether you are giving someone your phone number in dating or your email in business, it needs to seem worth it to you. You have to understand what is in it for you and what value you will receive from giving your information away. No one wants to be spammed in the business world and no one wants to be bombarded with unnecessary calls and texts in the dating world.

One of the most popular ways to get your ideal client's email is in an exchange for a lead magnet, also known as a free resource. The idea is to pull your ideal client in with your lead, like a magnet.

A lead magnet is usually a PDF guide, checklist, quiz, cheat sheet, template, mini e-book, roadmap, three-day challenge, how to ___, or a mini training/masterclass. You want to capture your ideal client's first and last name and email in exchange for this piece of valuable information. Your email list is a huge asset in your business. Social media followers could go away at any time, or your system could crash. An email list is yours forever and you get to control it.

Pro tips when creating your lead magnets:

- Don't give away all your gold but don't be afraid to give away anything at all. Just as you would keep a first date light, keep your free information light too. We don't want to scare them away.

  - When you give good value away, it earns people's trust and that is why someone is going to hire you. It's because they trust you! They might say to themselves "Oh if she can solve this problem for me, I bet she really can help me achieve ___" OR "If the first date was this good, I wonder what a 2nd date or mini vacation would be like?"

  - Free stuff answers the WHAT and the WHY and paid stuff answers the HOW or the detailed step-by-step!

- Have the end in mind when you are creating it. What is the big outcome your client is looking to get?

  - What is a quick win you can get them or what is a precursor they need to know or understand before working with you?

  - What is an objection you can proactively overcome

for them?

- The easiest thing to do is just pick one problem they are struggling with and give them five solutions to their problem. Now, you aren't telling them exactly how to solve it with detailed step-by- step instructions. Instead, you are just telling them WHAT they need to do to solve it.

- Make your title clear, concise, and compelling. Speak to their desire or pain. Have a subtitle that convinces them to read it. Always pretend your ideal client is thinking, "What is in it for me?"

- Keep the content short and sweet. It's not the time to get super deep or clinical.

- Showcase your brand. Include your biography, credibility statements, reasons you are different, and brief description of the services you offer.

- Make it easy for them to buy from you by including a call to action leading them to your calendar or service/product page.

Nurture

Once you get yourself in front of your ideal client, grab their attention, spark a conversation, and exchange information, it's time to keep moving them forward in the client journey. The goal is to nurture your potential client into becoming a paying customer.

Just like dating, the goal is to get to know one another well enough to see if it makes sense spending more time together and being together long term.

A sales pipeline looks at the different steps in the sales process, from gaining the lead to closing the sale. A potential client will either be a cold, warm, or hot lead in the pipeline.

Cold Leads: Cold leads are those who haven't yet expressed interest in the products or services of your business. They are positioned at the very beginning of the sale process. Most likely, they might have already given you their contact information and been introduced to your brand, but they are still in the evaluation, prospecting, and awareness phase. They are probably asking themselves; Do I like what they are saying? Do I feel a connection? Will they help me better myself? This is just as someone would in dating.

The goal with cold leads is to build trust, add value, and create interest for your services. One of the quickest ways to build the know, like, trust factor with a cold lead is to send them a sequence of emails. This will help them stay engaged and clearly see the value you have to offer, right off the bat. Your newest leads tend to be the most engaged so it's important to create momentum while you can. If you don't have an engaged community or they don't see the value whether it be in your free Facebook™ group, social media, or email marketing then they aren't going to give you the time of day and they certainly aren't going to buy from you. Only a third of your contacts buy almost immediately. The other percentage of people need to be given more information, followed up with, and nurtured. Lead nurturing can help develop relationships and turn cold leads into warm leads, thus increasing your chances of conversion.

Warm Leads: As in the name, warm leads are those that are already warmed up to your services. They most likely know your brand well and consume your content regularly, hopefully looking forward to hearing from you either on your social media or your emails. In other words, you are on their radar. However, you still seem to be in the friend zone, and they aren't ready to pull the trigger on your product or service just yet. They do tend to be more receptive to hearing about your deals and promotions. In order to get out of the friend zone, you need to proactively overcome their objections and show them what is possible when they start investing time, energy, and money into the problem you can help them solve. You need to help them fully trust you. Sharing client testimonials or answers to frequently asked questions with warm leads is a great strategy to move them forward in the client journey.

Hot Leads: Hot leads are where the money is because they are practically ready to make a purchase. They are qualified clients who have taken action, trust you, and indicated that they are very interested in investing. Perhaps they just need one last nudge to make the purchase. Hot leads have already identified their needs and how your business can help them resolve the issues they have plus they are actively looking for solutions. The goal with a hot lead is to provide them the necessary last bit of information they need in order to make a buying decision. They are typically looking for more details such as structure of your program, time commitment and financial investment. In addition, you might need to overcome any last objections they have and ensure they understand your ability to deliver the results you say you will. Oftentimes, all of this happens on a free consultation call.

Your Pipeline

A sales pipeline is an organized, visual way of tracking potential buyers as they progress through different stages in the purchasing process. You must learn how to fill your pipeline and keep it full at all times. A common phrase is "your pipeline is your lifeline." Essentially, if you don't have any cold, warm, or hot leads then you won't have any sales at all. Running a profitable and sustainable business means people need to be in the pipeline at all times; it's a long-term game.

The stages of a sales pipeline can help you and your team visualize your sales process. This visual representation portrays where in the sales funnel your potential clients are. You will be responsible for tracking them from one stage to the next as they move through the sales process.

For example, you might have stages that say: cold, warm, hot, booked a call, and signed up. As you grow, you can get more granular with the stages of the sales process. (Lahmi, 2022)

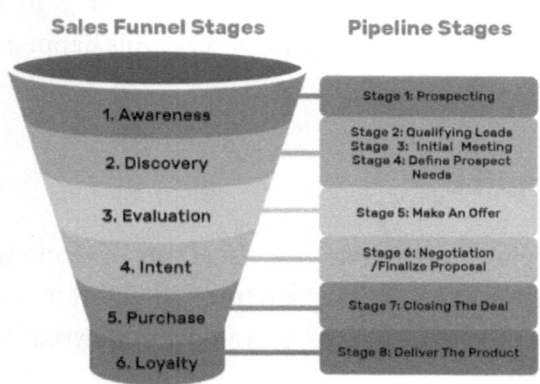

Stay Organized

As your business grows it will be critically important to stay organized and track your leads. You will need to know how many cold, warm, and hot leads you have as well as make internal notes of the interactions you have had with each prospect. This is the value of having a customer relationship management system (CRM). Think of it as an electronic health record system (EHR) for your sales process. A CRM system will allow you to streamline your process and easily manage your relationships with your future clients and current clients.

Numbers and data will be your lifeline when something goes sideways. If you don't have data, then you won't be able to diagnose the issue that led to the downfall.

Eventually you can set up marketing automations where your system can automatically tag leads as cold, warm, and hot. You can also have the software automatically send out emails, update contact information, and send you alerts. This will ensure that no leads slip through the cracks. If you can't track and evaluate the behavior of your potential clients, then you won't be able to determine what marketing steps you need to take next in order to turn a prospect into a paying client. You wouldn't expect a complete stranger to purchase your high-ticket course just as you wouldn't expect a stranger to say yes to marrying you. You need to know where your relationship stands with each of your leads before determining your next nurturing step.

There are many different CRM systems that will allow you to track your customer relationship and automations. It's never too early to invest in one. Most of the time it takes a bit of time to learn the ins and outs of the system, so starting to play around with the system sooner than later is never a bad idea. However, prior to getting my first CRM, I just used Excel spreadsheets to manually track the potential clients information and it did just fine. You will want to track client contact information, where they are in the sales pipeline (cold, warm, hot lead), conversations had, marketing metrics, revenue tracking, and appointment status. By tracking this information in an excel spreadsheet, you can gain valuable insights in your coaching business and improve your sales and marketing strategies.

Paid or Organic

There are many different types of marketing such as search engine marketing, email marketing, content marketing, social media marketing, influencer marketing, partnership marketing, affiliate marketing, TV, radio, mail marketing, outdoor marketing, and so on.

Most people will get in front of their audience in one of two ways, organic or paid. They are both different beasts to master that harness different goals. In order to scale, you must be able to implement both. However, in the foundation and growth stage of starting a coaching business, a hybrid strategy is not necessary and it's smart to start with organic first. Most successful businesses and brands will still push out organic content even when they implement paid advertising. It's a critical skill to learn especially when you are working on establishing your brand's personality and voice. Brand awareness is the first step in any customer's journey.

Organic

From a digital marketing lens, organic marketing is the act of creating and sharing free quality content in a way where your targeted audience can discover it. Content is something someone can read, listen to, or watch for inspiration, education, or entertainment. The goal is to nurture relationships and build connections. In the online world this could mean live trainings, webinars, podcasts, blogs, infographics, emails, reels, social media posts, and so much more.

If you are building a business without an online presence, then it would mean going to networking events, coffee dates, or having informational calls in order to organically meet people. Consistency is key when it comes to organic marketing. You want to stay top of mind so when it comes time for a consumer to make a buying decision, you are their first choice. It often takes time and testing to determine what works best for your audience and niche in order to start yielding results. In simple terms, organic marketing is all about building relationships by sharing informative, entertaining, and/or inspiring content to engage potential clients at every stage of their buying journey.

As a brand, when you post organically to your account, you can expect that the people who will see it are:

- A percentage of your followers (your 'organic reach')

- Your followers' followers (if people share your post)

- People following any hashtags you use

- People the algorithm pushes your content out to

When creating an online organic marketing strategy, it's important to know what social media channels you will focus on and what content you will be posting. Posting content can help you build credibility, add value, answer questions, spark interest, remove objections and drive potential customers to buy.

"Content builds relationships. Relationships are built on trust. Trust builds revenue."- Andrew Davis

The more places you post, the higher chances of it reaching your potential clients. I always say, if you don't feel like you are repeating yourself then you probably aren't saying it enough. Repurposing is key. You can take the same thing you posted last week and post it again; no one will remember. You can also take the same piece of content and post it multiple places with a slightly different image or order. In addition, you can take a larger or longer piece of content and chunk it up into multiple smaller pieces of content. Keep it simple for yourself. Copy and paste, copy and paste.

No one likes to be ghosted and in order to stay top of mind you need to be consistent. In order to be consistent, you should have a schedule for when your content will go out, what type of content will go out each day, and you should be batching it ahead of time, so you don't have to stress. You can even use an automated schedule so you don't have to manually post each day of the week. Creating content is easier than ever these days with artificial intelligence. There is no excuse to not be posting.

Pro tip: Do a weekly live training on one single topic your ideal clients would be interested in. Keep it the same day and time each week and record it for those who can't attend the live. It doesn't have to be fancy or long, keep it simple. If you are providing valuable content, your potential customers should start to view this like their favorite TV show. They can't wait for the next episode and if they have prior obligations, they can't wait to watch the recording and catch up. It's an added bonus for your ideal client to see you live on video because Forbes studies have shown that the average viewer retains 95% of a message when they watch it, as opposed to a mere 10% retention rate when reading it. (Stafford, 2017) Video can also get your audience to connect and communicate with you on a deeper emotional level. More so than words or pictures. It also helps people develop greater trust as people can see the intent and the face behind the brand. Hate it or love it, video content is here to stay. In fact, video is now the preferred medium for consuming information for a majority of Internet users. At the end of your live training, you can invite your audience to a free consultation call to see if working together would make sense. It's a great way to convert warm or hot leads into paying customers.

I have done plenty of live trainings where no one showed up. I could have given up, but I didn't, and I can't tell you how many people have messaged me saying how helpful my trainings have been and said they were binge watching replays or have been lurking for quite some time. You never know who is watching.

The content you post shouldn't only be for consistency, it should be intentional to convert. The topics you post should aim to solve the problems your ideal client is having. It should also aim to stop the scroll and connect with them emotionally by hitting their pain and/or desire. Best practice is to always have a call to action telling your potential client exactly what you want them to do next. Your calls to action may differ for your cold, warm, and hot leads which is why it's important to have an effective plan and track your client relationships.

Here is an example of the PAS (problem, agitate, solve) copywriting framework for a weight loss/intuitive eating coach. This is one of the most popular copywriting frameworks there is.

Problem: Have you ever tried a diet only to find that the weight comes back as soon as you stop restricting your food intake? Or worse, do you find yourself feeling guilty and ashamed when you "cheat" on your diet, leading to a never-ending cycle of self-punishment and yo-yo dieting?

Agitate: The truth is, diets don't work. Research shows that the majority of people who lose weight on a diet will regain it within a few years, and some will even end up weighing more than when they started. Not only that, but the constant focus on what you can't eat can lead to feelings of deprivation, binging, and even disordered eating.

Solve: There is a better way. By learning to listen to your body's natural hunger and fullness cues, and by focusing on nourishing your body with whole, unprocessed foods that you enjoy, you can ditch the diet mentality and build a healthier relationship with food and your body. As a coach who helps women feel more confident in their bodies, I can guide you on this journey and provide the support you need to make lasting change.

CTA (call to action): Please comment "ditch the diet" if you'd like to learn more about how I can help you!

There are many other proven copywriting frameworks that you can use to post on social media with strategy.

Partnerships are another great way to connect with potential clients. Oftentimes, this can be free. The point is to leverage someone else's audience with a give and take strategy. Strategic partnership marketing is about building a relationship that is mutually beneficial. Examples are speaking to their audience via podcasts or educational content, lead magnet exchange, driving traffic to your service by leveraging email lists, and collaboration posts and shoutouts on social media.

With all the social media channels out there, Facebook™ is still the number one platform with almost three billion users.

This is why my proprietary client attraction system and modern marketing masterplan has a heavy emphasis on leveraging and monetizing Facebook™ groups. I will speak more on this further on.

Paid

Paid advertising typically consists of running ads to your targeted audiences who are likely to be interested, either through boosting your organic content or designing new unique advertisements.

Not only can paid advertising help you raise brand awareness and attract new followers like organic marketing, it can help you promote your newest service, generate leads, and most importantly drive conversions.

It allows you to get in front of your target audience much more quickly and also allows you to reach a larger audience. In turn, this will help you reach your business goals quicker. However, doing things the quick way isn't always the smartest.

Paid advertising is a highly complex field of expertise. The key to mastering paid advertising is testing. Think of it as an experiment that has hundreds of variables that could impact your ideal outcome. You will want to track and test the engagement and conversion rate of your ad. Some of the things you will be testing within your ad is the audiences, platforms, content, graphics, and messaging. You want to identify what works best before allocating a large budget to your ad campaigns. It will take both time and money to figure out what is working and what isn't working. Not to mention, there are quite a few semi-complicated technology steps you will need to take in order to properly set up and track your paid ads. This is why I do not recommend prematurely jumping into paid advertising when you are setting up the foundation of your business. There are a ton of other moving parts you will be focusing on.

It's also important to have realistic expectations when it comes time to implementing paid advertising into your marketing plan. We live in an age where a lot of things tend to be guaranteed instantly but paid advertising is not always the magic wand people tend to make it out to be. It's not as simple as flicking on the light switch and having an influx of eager clients knocking on your door. The proper amount of time and budget needs to be allocated in conjunction with a consistent and well proven strategy.

To keep it simple, paid advertising is a great tool. I use it myself in my own business. I love it. However, just like anything else, there is a time and place for it and when you do decide to implement it into your marketing strategy, you need to be able to track the key performance indicators to make sure realistic expectations are set.

Competitor Research

Previously, we talked about what makes you the Beyoncé of your space, what makes you special and what expertise you are bringing to the table. The second part of being the Beyoncé of your space comes from competitor research.

Before I dive into competitor research, I'd like to set the tone for my intention of this section because I actually hate the word competition when it's used in this entrepreneurial space. I'm a big fan of collaboration instead of competition. With one of my core values being abundance, I believe there is room for everyone. Anyone who is doing something similar to you is really just helping you complete your mission much faster. We are all connected. A tree wouldn't compete with a tree. Ecosystems are just like communities, and they don't compete with one another. Instead, they communicate, collaborate, and cooperate. Something we could all probably do more of.

My intention is not for you to fall into a lack mindset when studying your quote-on-quote competition, but instead it's to understand that competitor research within your specific market is a foundational principle of marketing when understanding why a customer chooses to buy your product or service. It's also a great way to understand your business strengths and weaknesses.

Here are some questions you should ask yourself when conducting competitor research.

- How do you do it better?

- How do you do it differently?

- What do you include that they don't?

- What are the price differences?

- How does the user experience differ?

- How do your marketing strategies differ?

- Are users engaged? If so, why/how?

As you know, the market is always changing and evolving. Therefore, competitor research is something that should be done continuously. When you keep tabs on your competitors it will be much easier to strategize how your own business can aim to improve.

Pro tip: Don't get so caught up in consuming that you forget to create. Create more than you consume.

Modern Marketing Masterplan

I used to hate Facebook™ with a passion so what I am about to tell you is comical to me.

Do you want to know what I believe is the most effective way to build an amazing, value driven community that converts quality leads into paying customers?

You guessed it, it's Facebook™ groups.

This isn't my opinion alone. Majority of the successful six, seven, and eight figure earners will tell you that Facebook™ groups are currently the number one sales asset you can use to build trust and authority with your potential clients. It's also a wonderful way to fill your pipeline with pre-qualified prospects who are ready to purchase your signature coaching program.

Basically, the more people who join your group, the more money you'll make. Think of your free Facebook™ group as your money making, client getting group. It's a hub of potential clients who opted in to listen to you speak on your area of expertise. How cool is that?

When people join your group and see you as the tribe leader of hundreds and thousands of people, who are all in your community for education and inspiration around the topic that is your exact expertise, your word carries more weight, and you automatically earn more trust. As you know, trust equals conversions.

Trust building has always been important when it comes to sales, but I would say it's even more important these days with the saturated coaching industry. Regardless of your niche, people are more protective over whom they choose to work with than ever before. It's a possibility that your potential client could be shopping around for other similar coaches. It's also a possibility that your potential client could be afraid to part with their money again given their last experience with a coach.

As a business owner, it's important to understand and accept the skepticism and constantly ask yourself how you can continue to build trust with your potential clients and overcome their objections.

Hint: Your Facebook™ group is a great way to continually build trust!

Let's break it down. Growth plus content equals monetization.

Growth: Growing your group and audience size is incredibly important. Your newest members are always the most excited so it's important to constantly gain new members to keep engagement up. So, how will you get potential clients inside your group? You will first need to know where they are hanging out and then you'll invite them. As mentioned earlier, you can do organic marketing or paid advertising in order to invite potential clients to your group. Regardless, you will want to give them a reason to join. Tell them what is in it for them and why they should join. What are they going to get out of it? Make it compelling! Be specific!

You can use other social media platforms as a funnel to drive people to your free Facebook™ community. The behavior is very different on all social media platforms. Some platforms are meant for scrolling and some platforms are meant for conversations and engaging. Every audience is different, and every business owner has their preference. There is no right or wrong answer when it comes to the best platform. However, there is no doubt that Facebook™ groups allow coaches to create a more intimate and interactive community around their service, which can help build trust and loyalty with potential clients. When new members come into your group, they will need to answer three approval questions. They will look something like this, but within your niche.

Question 1

This group is only for female clinicians who have a business and are looking to add coaching or already provide coaching. Are you a business owner and a clinician looking to add coaching or grow your coaching business?

☐ Yes

☐ No

Edit　　　　　　　　　　Delete

Question 2

What is your email address (type it accurately) so I can send you my freebie (3 simple steps to add coaching and 3x your therapy income)? Your email will be used to send you materials we think you'll love to help your business thrive. Opt out anytime

Write your answer...

Edit　　　　　　　　　　Delete

Question 3

Would you like to learn more about working with me to help you achieve more money and impact more lives by creating your own signature coaching program?

☐ Yes

☐ No

All three of these questions will help you pre-qualify your leads. If someone is not your ideal client, they should read your questions and decide not to join. If they are your ideal client, then you just scored big by collecting their email address and understanding if they are curious about what you have to offer. If they answer yes to wanting to learn more about working with you then they are essentially saying yes to having a conversation with you about your services. However, this does not mean you should just send them a link straight away to your service page or calendar.

New members aren't usually ready to buy right off the bat. You need to first build rapport and have a genuine conversation with them. They might also want to look around at all the valuable content you have to offer. In order to match them with the right piece of content, you can ask them what they are struggling with most right now and then tag them in a previous training you did on that exact topic. Tagging your potential clients in content that will proactively answer their questions and handle their objections will also save you a lot of time and energy replying to messages. After you've tagged them, you shouldn't just hope and pray they consume the content and come back to you. Instead, you should be proactive and continuously follow up to see how they enjoyed it and if they had any questions.

Fortune is in the follow up. Keep the conversation going. Your goal is to figure out if they are indeed a good fit for your service or not. You will need to ask a series of questions to figure this out. How serious are they? How soon are they looking to make this change? Are they looking for professional support when it comes to solving their problem(s)? Do they have the funds and time to invest? You will need to figure all of this out prior to inviting them to a call. The last thing you want in your business is time sucking 45-minute sales calls with prospects who aren't serious or aren't a good fit. The best way to quickly discern if they are going to be a good fit for a call or not is to get them on a short 10 min call, also known as a triage call, so you can uncover their needs, discuss how you could help, and build a deeper level of rapport. It can look like this, "Based on everything you've said, I'm pretty confident I can help but I have a few more questions and sometimes it's easier and faster if we just hop on a quick call. Do you happen to have five minutes?"

Pro tip: When a new member comes in, give them a warm welcome with high energy, just as you would if someone came to your house for your dinner party. Give them the lay of the land by tagging them in an informational welcome post that tells them exactly what they can expect in your group and how to get the most out of it. Be a good hostess.

Content: Do not post about anything and everything, making your group a free for all. Cut the fluff. Less is more and quality is much more important than quantity. Don't post so much information that it gets lost and your paid program becomes unnecessary. You need to post with a value driven strategy and have a consistent schedule, so your audience stays engaged. For example, I post a poll every Monday inside my Therapist to Coach Accelerator ™ group asking what topic my audience wants me to teach on Wednesday for the live stream training. They know that Wednesday is the day I do my live stream training and that I do it at the same time every week. Other things I post are my lead magnets, or freebies, testimonials, and posts speaking to my clients' pain points, desires, and objections. All this content is evergreen and can be repurposed inside the group to continue to provide value.

Unless you are running a promotion or holiday sale of sorts, I want you to remember that you aren't selling anything inside of your group. Amazon is where people go to buy things. Facebook™ is where people go for community. Facebook™ is a social platform where people want to have conversations. Therefore, the only thing you are doing inside your group is providing valuable content and generating conversations around it. Your goal is to build likeability and trust with your potential clients. From there, they will very quickly start to understand that you know how to solve their problem and from there they will metaphorically raise their hand and want to know more about working with you, especially when you invite them to raise their hand by inviting them to a call with you.

Pro tip: Don't rely solely on the Facebook™ algorithm for reach. Instead, use email marketing to point your clients back to your posts within your group to ensure you are getting the greatest number of eyes on any given post.

Here are some of the most common questions I get regarding setting up your lead generation Facebook™ group:

- What do I name my group? Make it clear and concise. Call out to the population you plan to work with and the outcome you will get them. Keep it simple.

- What if my ideal client isn't on Facebook™? Think again. Facebook™ is still the number one platform with three billion monthly users.

What if my group members are ghosting me? Rejection is part of the coaching game. It's very possible that the member did not accept your friend request and your message didn't make it to their direct inbox. It's also a possibility that they are silent lurkers. Like I mentioned earlier, I can't tell you how many times I've had group members join the Therapist to Coach Accelerator™ program and say, "I'm finally ready. I've been following along with your content for months." Do your best to follow up but if you are getting ghosted, don't take it personally.

- How much time does it take to run my group? As much

or as little time as you want. Personally, I post two to three times a week in my group. I have a team, so I do not spend more than three hours a week in my group, and it's still highly engaged. If you want to leverage your time, I'd suggest scheduling out your posts and hiring a team to accept/deny members and have conversations on your behalf.

It's possible that a simple Facebook™ group could be the sales and marketing asset you've been looking for to book yourself solid, gain consistent results, and scale.

In general, the key to successful lead generation through Facebook™ groups is to provide value to members, foster engagement and conversation, and build relationships with potential clients.

I dare you to give it a try!

PS: Join the Therapist to Coach Accelerator Facebook™ group and see how I run mine. Hint, hint, it's the same way I teach you to run yours!

Recap:

Marketing is like dating. You have to find your ideal client, get noticed, build rapport, have a conversation, and exchange information.

Don't be afraid to give away free value. It earns trust. I hope you are enjoying this free value and I'm earning your trust right now. Wink-wink.

Stay organized and know where your clients are in the sales process.

Everything comes down to organic marketing or paid advertising.

Study your competition with an abundance mindset.

Use Facebook™ groups to your advantage!

Chapter 5

Sales

Say your offer with confidence and conviction and learn how to sell with my secret soul-aligned techniques so you don't have to feel salesy. Kiss imposter syndrome and the haters goodbye as you step into your dream coaching business.

People wake up every day ready to pay for a solution to their problem. People hire coaches for three reasons. They can't do it on their own, they want to do it faster, or they want to follow a proven system.

If you run a business, and you can't master sales, then it will cost you your whole business.

The word sales always triggers people's emotions. Some look at it with disgust and despair, while others look at it as an opportunity, challenge, or form of compassion. I would say most people who look at sales as icky or slimy do so only because they had a bad experience getting sold to. Rarely, do people look at all of their enjoyable sales experiences. The experiences where they bought something so seamlessly and without a doubt because it was probably already something they were thinking about purchasing for a while.

Here is the deal. We have slimy selling, and we have true sacred soul aligned selling. Slimy or sleazy selling is convincing. Convincing means we are getting people to take action because it benefits us. Yuck.

Sacred soul aligned selling is persuasion. Persuasion is helping someone make a decision that they already know they want to make. When we add on the soul aligned piece, it's helping someone make a decision that is in their best interest, that they know they want to make. I mention best interest because someone could love your offer and want it even if it's not right for them. For example, I get a ton of newbie clinicians wanting to take the Therapist to Coach Accelerator™ program. It's enticing for them to make more money and have a larger impact. However, in order to be successful in the program, you have to have enough experience to be able to create a coaching curriculum to get someone from problem to solution. Oftentimes this comes with years of clinical experience. If a clinician was just starting to see clients for the first time, it would not be in their best interest to attempt to create a signature coaching program for a specific population. Just because your offer is bomb, doesn't mean it's bomb for everyone.

The process of a service meeting a prospect or a client, who ends up investing in the value because they see its worth, is called sales. I don't understand what is there to hate in this entire process. Sales isn't something you do to someone, it's something you do for and with someone. It's a noble profession.

In order for your business to have what is necessary to solve your clients' problems, you need to have resources. In order to have resources you need to have money. The money you ask for is needed to apply the necessary resources to solve your client's problem; it's simply an energy exchange. Paying is noble too. When someone is effective at sales, it's truly a win-win.

Learning to sell is a skill. It can be learned. Believe it or not, therapists are actually fantastic at it because rapport is their middle name and rapport is always the number one thing that makes or breaks the sale.

Say It with Confidence and Conviction

Your offer is freaking bomb. I know it is. You created your offer stack that speaks to all the solutions your client is longing for. You have bonuses and a guarantee. The perceived value is so high, your clients understand that they are getting a steal! Plus, it's so specifically curated just for them! It's literally the best in class offer. You know it and I need you to own it.

If you don't believe in your offer, no one will. You must know and believe on a very deep level that what you are offering is going to transform so many lives.

I think I can safely speak for all of us when I say we didn't get into this field to make money, right? I know your intentions are pure. I know you aren't selling your coaching program to make a quick buck. I know that your heart and soul want to help the world. So, remind yourself of that! Bring this energy and passion when you are having a conversation with a prospective client. Money will show up after, it's a magnifier.

Imposter Syndrome

Surprisingly, 80-90% of people have it. As we know, it's not in the DSM. It's not an actual syndrome. It's more of a phenomenon. The phenomenon that a high achieving individual will be seen as a fraud.

It can show up in business like this...

- Attributing success to luck

- Attributing your success to someone else

- Not taking compliments well

- Perfectionism/overworking

- Spending more time on projects

- Not feeling intelligent enough

- Feeling fear about success

- Overestimating others while underestimating oneself

- Self-sabotage to cover the feelings of inadequacy

- Feeling the need to prove yourself

- Feeling like you're still working on it yourself so who are you to teach it

You might say things to yourself like:

- "Who am I to teach them about X, Y, or Z?"

- "Who am I to sell this program at X price?" "Who am I to be a coach?"

- "Do I actually know what I'm talking about?"

- "Who is going to listen to me and believe me?"

Sound familiar?

If you are struggling with any of those things, I want you to ask yourself why you're struggling? What will make you not feel like an imposter? What is making you feel like an imposter? Is it an outcome? I could bet money it is.

When you finally hit a specific revenue, when you finally have a specific number of clients, when your course is finally done, when you have a specific number of members, followers or whatever, then will you have made it or be successful? Will this finally make you not feel like a fraud?

If this is the case, you are being way too outcome oriented and it's leaving you unable to focus on the process itself. Release the outcome and do the action.

This is just the ego trying to rip you out of the present moment and drag you to a future time. It's the ego treating the present moment like an obstacle, convincing you that the grass is greener on the other side.

So, what do you do about it? You bring yourself back to the facts. The fact that you can solve a problem for your client. The fact that you can get your client to the outcome they desire. This is what matters. Remember you don't have to solve ALL the problems your client is having. You aren't a god, guru, or genie. Your experience means you've already gained the necessary skills and strategies to overcome the struggles your clients are dealing with. You are many steps ahead. Dissociate your feelings from the outcome you provide.

The imposter cycle can go on and on if it's not recognized or interrupted. It looks something like this. First you have your trigger. Whatever activity you are doing has a lot of potential for you to make mistakes. It's probably something new or something big. You are putting pressure on yourself, and the performance anxiety is real. Then comes the behavior. You act in one of two ways. You either overwork to cover up fear of feeling like a fraud or you procrastinate what you know you need to do. Possibly it's a mixture of both. From there, you'll get a performance review of sorts. You will either give yourself a review, or a coach or mentor will give you one. Ultimately, you'll get validation that the actions you took were okay, but you might obsess over the constructive criticism or mistakes. Because you are high achieving you won't internalize the fact that what you did was okay. You don't internalize the approval. This leads you back to the beginning of the vicious cycle with a different trigger.

Pro-tips to interrupt the imposter cycle:

Allow yourself to be a work in progress.

- Imagine Steve Jobs never came out with the iPhone I because he wanted it to be perfect?

- Be okay starting at average as you grow into exceptional.

- You will always get better and do better so give yourself grace.

- Do imperfect action, it's better than no action. You're building muscle.

- Ask yourself, what did I learn from this experience, instead of what did I do wrong

Remember getting specific and going narrow is actually key.

- When you are trying to create a program to help someone with their life or relationships, you may think "well I can't solve all their problems and fix all of their relationships or life" and then you feel like a fraud.

- You aren't supposed to fix all their problems. Pick one you are confident in.

Kick the comparisons

- Abundance mindset! There is room for everyone to be successful. You are right where you are supposed to be.

- If you are jealous of someone else's success, you have a desire for more success. That is fabulous.

- Use other people's success as evidence. If they can do it, you can too.

- Give yourself credit for what you have accomplished. You're going to have a dopamine hit, feel motivated and want to make more progress. Progress attracts more progress.

Remember how powerful you are!

- None of your success showed up because of luck. Even if something was a complete synchronicity, and you can't conceptualize how you got there, it doesn't mean you are a fraud. Remember that we are always energetic matches for the things we welcome into our lives. You aren't new at manifesting. Everything up until this point in your life is because you manifested it consciously or subconsciously. You are powerful as fuck.

Ask yourself, do I actually have imposter syndrome or am I just fearful or unprepared when it comes to taking action towards success? Do you actually feel like a fraud and struggle with all of those things I talked about earlier, or are you just fearing taking action or feel unprepared to take action? There is a big difference.

Some people walk around telling themselves that they have imposter syndrome just because it is a common thing we talk about in today's world. Pay attention to the stories you are telling yourself. The last thing you want to do is self-sabotage your success.

No one can make you feel inferior without your consent. – Eleanor Roosevelt

Sales is a Skill

Most people teach sales psychology based on words and scripts alone and although these can be good, they can also be absolutely horrible and robotic. Words are only 7% of rapport. How you speak those words, your tonality, volume, temp, rhythm, and pitch account for 38% of communication. The remaining 55% of communication is the result of your physiology, sometimes referred to as body language and includes facial expressions, eye contact, posture, stance, composure, movements, and breathing patterns. This means that how you deliver your message and how you present yourself carries more weight than your words itself. You will want to match and mirror your client's tonality and physiology in order to maintain rapport throughout the call. It's important to note that matching and mirroring should be done subtly and authentically. It's important to adapt your communication style to the situation and the needs of the potential client, rather than relying too heavily on matching and mirroring as a one-size-fits-all technique.

Every action a prospect makes is motivated by improvement. People buy because they believe it will enhance their lives somehow. Some of the basic needs motivating them to buy might be money, security, being liked, status and prestige, health and fitness, praise and recognition, power, influence, leadership, love, and companionship. Determining the prospect's motivator is a crucial sales skill you will want to master.

People don't buy on logic; they buy on emotion, and then justify their decision with logic. They buy with their hearts, not their heads. If you can build an emotional connection between you and your prospects, you will succeed in sales. Practice building this muscle.

Sales Call

A sales call process can be compared to the process of going to the doctor. When you go to the doctor, they ask you a ton of questions to determine the problem, if there is one. Then they give you a recommendation for your problem and discuss the details of the recommendation. Finally, you get to decide if the recommendation is best for you or not.

The first thing you will want to do on a sales call is build rapport. Break the ice and just shoot the shit for a minute. Ask them where they are calling in from. Talk about the weather. Find a common ground. Give a compliment. Make a joke about your love hate relationship with technology if there was an issue getting connected. Be a relatable human.

The second thing you'll want to do is frame the call. Take the lead back and set the agenda. It will look something like this.

"I'm so excited for today's call. The whole purpose is for me to understand you and your situation better and for me to explain to you what it is that I do. From there, we can come to a conclusion if working together would make sense. Regardless, I'm confident that I will be able to help you in some way and will be able to point you in the right direction. So, let's dive in, shall we? If you don't mind, we can start with you and dive into your current situation and you can tell me more about it and where you would like to be instead, your goals! Then I can answer any questions you have and tell you more about my program. Ultimately, we will see if it makes sense to work together. Sound good?"

Framing the call will help your prospective client feel at ease and ensure you are starting off the call on the same page.

Your job is to figure out four things.

1. What is not working for them?

2. What is their true problem?

3. What is their problem costing them?

4. What is their motivation to solve it?

Pretend like you are a really curious detective and ask the following questions! After these questions you should have a real understanding of your prospective client's life and problems in relation to the area you help people within.

- What led you to this point of finally reaching out?

- What is the big outcome you are looking for?

- What do you mean specifically?

- What are the problems?

- How exactly is this showing up for you?

- How bad is it?

- Why do you think that is?

- How long has this been going on?

- Is it impacting your family, relationships, confidence, health, finances?

- Tell me more.

- Is it costing you time and energy?

- What have you tried that didn't work? Have you tried anything?

- How bad do you want a solution out of this?

- Are you seriously ready for a change?

- Do you want this change now?

- Can you afford to not make a change?

- What are you missing out on?

- What will your life continue to be like if you don't make this change?

- What is the dream come true?

- What will your life look like specifically when you achieve the big outcome?

You should approach the conversation with a judgment-free curious attitude. You never want the client to feel bad for vulnerably sharing their problems. You also don't want to go into telling your own personal story, unless they ask. Keep it about them.

After the information gathering, it's time to do a brief recap to ensure everyone is on the same page again. This will let your prospective client know that you truly understand where they are right now.

It could look something like this.

"Thank you so much for sharing all of that. If it's alright with you I'd like to do a quick recap to ensure I'm not missing anything. So, I understand your big goal is _ _ _ _ _ so that you can finally feel _ _ _ _ _ and be able to do _ _ _ _. But right now, you are currently experiencing_ _ _ _ symptoms from _ _ _ _ situation and it's impacting you because _ _ _ _ _ _. You've had a hard time with _ _ _ _ _ and it's left you feeling _ _ _ _. You sort of feel held back by_ _ _ _ but you don't want it to stop you because more than anything you really desire (big outcome). Am I right? What did I miss?"

After confirming the information and ensuring you are on the same page, it's your turn to share your offer and explain how you have helped plenty of people just like them. Let them know that they are not alone, they are in the right place, and you can help. Reiterate your area of expertise and how specifically you work to solve the problems they have. This can be done by sharing your offer stack with them as well as client success stories. Oftentimes, you might have the urge to provide them with tangible tips and skills they could implement right away in order to solve their problem, it's just the therapist in you. However, now is not the time to give them advice and teach them. It's the time to share your offer and tell them how you could teach them tangible tips and skills if they decide to go deeper. Make sense?

Once you've shared your offer as a recommendation, you can ask them if they have any questions? At this point, they will most likely ask you about next steps and what it would look like to work together. This is where you will provide logistical details and investment options.

Notice how I used the word investment. I didn't say price or cost. Psychologically speaking, when people hear the word cost, fee, rate, or price they think expense instead of investment. Investment on the other hand implies a return. You always want your prospective client to be focusing on the return they are going to get from your amazing program.

When you explain the logistics of time and financial investment, your prospective client might have objections. I'm going to teach you how to overcome these objections in a little bit.

Sales Call Pro tips:

- Do your homework ahead of time by reading their questionnaire or past conversations you've had with them.

- Have a pen and paper handy.

- Have your offer stack in front of you if you don't have it memorized.

- Have your payment plans ready.

- Take a deep breath and physically shake off the nerves before the call.

- Release the outcome. What is meant to be will be. This will allow you to be present instead of being distracted by your own "hidden agenda."

It's a Numbers Game

If your offer is $2,500 and you close two out of every four people you talk to, that's $5k every four consult calls you have. So, if you can get eight calls a month, which is two a week, you can close $10k every month. Take your monthly income goal and divide it by your program price and that equals how many clients you need per month. You will want to track how many calls you have per week, the percentage that show up, and the percentage that convert to paying clients. Consistently tracking your sales numbers and current process will help you understand the actions you need to take in order to hit your goals and which areas you can work on to improve your overall sales game.

Sales isn't only a numbers game. It's an effectiveness game too. Quality leads are much more important than quantity.

Pre-qualify

The last thing you want is a bunch of people booking on your free consultation calendar who aren't actually a fit for your service and who aren't serious about investing. The way to avoid this is to have a pre-qualifying/screening process. This can be done in many different ways, but it will always consist of asking your prospective client a series of questions. The most common screening process is through your call application. You can also do triage calls, or mini calls, prior to your full-blown consultation call. A short five to ten minute call will allow you to see if a longer consultation would even make sense. In addition, you can hire a setter who can have pre-qualifying conversations on your behalf and only set someone on your calendar if they are a good fit.

Regardless of how you pre-qualify, before you dedicate your time to a free consult call, you will want to ensure your prospective client matches your ideal client avatar description that you created back in Chapter 2. You will need to make sure they are coming to you for the problem that you specifically help with. You will also want to understand their level of urgency in order to solve this problem. How soon are they looking to invest in themselves, if at all? Additionally, you will want to discern their level of coachability. If a prospective client is questioning your proven process or seems stuck in their ways, they probably won't be a good fit for your coaching program.

The idea is to essentially get the sale before you even have the consult call. The call just seals the deal. Obtaining the sale before the call will come from strong messaging, ensuring your prospective client knows your niche, your offer, and the tangible quantifiable outcome that you provide. You will also want to proactively overcome their potential objections in your messaging.

If there is clarity and alignment from both the service provider and the prospect, the sale should be easy.

Handling Objections

Your objective is not to get your prospect to buy. It's to help them make the right decision. How you handle your prospects' objections will set the tone for what it would actually be like to work with you. You must hold them in this space, just as you would your coaching program. It's a really great way to display your coaching skills, build trust, and present with mastery.

Before a client says yes to your offer, they will always have some sort of debate in their head. It's normal and highly likely. Some of their objections are the truth and some are just BS excuses. Sometimes they are just missing a piece of valuable information.

There are four big objections that prospects tend to have, regardless of what niche you are in. If you can't overcome these four objections then your prospects won't realize that what you're selling is exactly what they are looking for, the awaited solution to their problem.

1. **Money:** I can't afford it right now, I need to save up, it's more than I was expecting

2. **Time:** I don't have the time, kids' timing is interfering, I'm busy with something else need to finish that first

3. **Have to talk to someone else:** Need to talk to husband or partner

4. **Lack of belief:** I don't know if this will work for me, I need to think about it, what if I can't follow through, I can't do it on my own.

Let's address them one by one. Regardless of the objection, I will always encourage you to agree with your prospects' objection first. This will ensure you keep the rapport.

Money: If someone says that they can't afford it or it's too much money you should not abort mission. I repeat. Do not abort mission. You also shouldn't discount your price for this person or lower your prices in general. Your program is worth it. You aren't overcharging.

The first thing you should do is validate and agree. Agree first, always. Put yourself in their shoes. We want to be on the same side as our prospects. No arguing with them. This will also continue to keep the rapport and build trust. You want to be collaborative not combative. Confirm that concerns about money are real and you respect their money choices. "I completely understand that this is a big investment. We never want to put anyone in an uncomfortable financial situation. So, if now isn't the right time, that is totally fine. On the other hand, we never want money to be the reason someone can't invest in themselves."

Then you will want to ask permission to ask a few more questions so you can determine if they are just scared to invest the money or if they truly don't have it. If they do indeed have the money, they may be seeking permission that it's okay to invest in themselves or be looking for more information. You can say, "I get that this is a big investment and a big step, especially considering _ _ _ _ _. Tell me, is there anything you need to understand to take away any concern you might have?"

If they don't have the funds, you can help them get resourceful. There could be available resources and funds that they haven't thought about. Maybe they can afford one of your payment plans.

Regardless, you will want to keep the focus on the value your service provides and how it's different. Review the deliverables, features, benefits, and guarantee of your offer with a particular focus on their return on investment. You can also share client success stories.

Their problem will always be costing them. It's either costing them past pain, present pain, or future pain or perhaps costing them all three. You'll need to frame the value of your service in terms of what will happen if they don't solve the problem and what that will continue to cost them. Finally having the dream outcome is priceless. You can't even put a price tag on it.

You can ask if money is the only thing holding them back and if it weren't for the investment would they be a 10/10 ready and excited to be in your signature program. It's a possibility that this could bring up other objections such as time or belief.

Time: Your prospective client is either thinking they don't have the time to dedicate to your program or the timing in their life is just off right now. Just like money, they are either feeding you an excuse or it's a legit timing issue. Ask questions to find out.

They could just be assuming that the time investment is much bigger than it actually is. You can say, "Timing is everything, I totally get it. Actually, most of my clients (work full time, have kids, and have a lot going on) so I already have a solution for you. First, let me ask you how many hours a week can you dedicate to this work?"

Let them know they only need to dedicate five to seven hours per week to get results. That's an hour a day.

Most likely, this will help them see that they can indeed fit this into their busy life.

If they can't dedicate the five to seven hours per week then timing is definitely a valid concern. Have a discussion with them to see if you can help them move anything around in their schedule to make space for this. They might need to prioritize and cut back somewhere else in order to make space for your program.

If they cannot currently switch anything around and make space, ask them when they can and how far in the future do they see your program as a realistic option. This will help you understand when it's appropriate to professionally follow up with them again.

You can make the deal even sweeter by offering a fast action taker discount. Sometimes they just need a sweet incentive to take action now. You can offer a discount if they enroll within the next 24 hours. You can even allow them to push their start date out a few weeks. Therefore, they can capture the sweet discount now but still have time to get their ducks in a row before officially starting.

Have to Talk to Someone Else: I like to avoid this objection, when possible, by including a question on my call application form that asks, "Are you the sole decision maker of your investments?" They have the option to click yes or no, I will bring my partner to this call.

However, this objection can still come up. "I have to talk to my spouse."

If someone feels they won't get their desired results for the investment they have to make or does not understand the real-world value, then they may use the *I have to talk to my spouse* line as an out to not move forward with your program.

If it's not an out and they truly need to talk to their spouse about the investment and decision, as it probably impacts them somehow, then you have to respect this. You will want to know what exactly they want to speak to their spouse about. Is it the investment? The offer itself? The timing? What is it?

You can say, "I completely understand that you want to speak to your spouse. This is a big decision and quite literally life changing. I want them to be on board, too. I will send you a follow up email with everything we discussed, so you can reference it when speaking with them. If they have any questions, I'd love for the three of us to hop on a call again, and I can answer them! But, just so I know where you stand, is this something that you are wanting to move forward with?" You would want to know if their partner said yes then they would say yes.

If they say yes, then you can ask if they think their partner will support them in this decision. You can also ask if they have shared with their partner why they want to invest and how it will help them. Sometimes they have only gotten vulnerable and excited with you but not fully with their partner.

The answer to all these questions will help you determine the next step in the sales process. If they are wanting to move forward but just need to speak to their spouse, then try to get the follow up call booked in the calendar before you end the call.

Lack of Belief: It will be important for you to get down to the bottom of your prospects' lack of belief so you can help them with a mindset shift.

It's not just about your potential client liking, knowing and trusting you that will bring you the sale. They also have to believe that your service will help them get the desired result. They need to believe that your offer is the answer to their problem and see that it's worth the investment.

They also need to believe in themselves and that they can do it. They could just fear failure.

It's also a really big possibility that they might have been burned or jaded by another coach before and they are afraid to invest again thinking that this may not work for them. It feels dangerous, just like skydiving! They logically know the equipment is working and the parachute will bring them to the ground safely. They even saw other people go before them, but it still feels scary when they are about to jump. They might be tempted to continue to DIY because it seems safer to them. You will want to acknowledge their fear and assure them that your program is different and that they won't be left disappointed.

Having testimonials and clients' success stories/wins is one of the best ways to overcome this objection. Having a guarantee to lower the risk will also help them make the leap with confidence and ease.

Testing

When I first started my business, I had no idea that I would be spending so much time figuring out what didn't work just to figure out what does work. I felt like I was a little kid who kept falling off their bike.

In love, they say you must kiss a lot of toads before you find your prince and in business you have to try a lot of things that don't work in order to figure out your magic recipe for success.

Every business is different. Every entrepreneur is different. Every audience is different. No matter who you are and what type of business you run, you should always be testing. Entrepreneurship is like one massive science experiment.

Every business owner wants to know whether they are making the right choices or not, but you won't know until you test. You have to let the experiment run its course in order to collect data.

Sacred Soul Aligned Selling

We are all here to serve in one way or another. To help each other. To unite. And on a spiritual level, to walk each other home.

Your soul equals the core of your being.

At the core of your being is your mission.

Your mission/purpose equals your passion met with the needs of others.

How beautiful is that?

What's even more beautiful is that abundance is your birthright if you follow your desire and purpose. Meaning you wouldn't have this desire or passion to begin with and it wouldn't have been created as part of you if you weren't supposed to receive abundance for it. When I say abundance, I don't just mean money. Abundance comes in many forms such as freedom, relationships, opportunities, flexibility, etc.

Sacred soul aligned selling is about sharing what you have to offer unapologetically and without any filter. It's pursuing your soul's mission relentlessly, knowing that it's going to help so many people.

You don't need to feel weird, guilty or salesy about completing and following through on your massive mission. You are sharing your genius. You aren't selling shit. You can't put a price tag on your genius. It's priceless but money is just an energy exchange and we do live in a 3D world. You have a life to live so you are putting a price tag on it.

Your intention is not to "sell," your intention is to inspire, heal, bring hope, and transform lives. It's to complete your soul's mission and be a heart centered leader. Selling is just the byproduct.

It sounds so cliche but the best business advice I can give you is to JUST BE YOU. Trying to replicate how other people speak and do business will not lead you down the path of abundance.

Now, I do think it's important to learn proven strategies that work but it's more important that you do it in a way that feels good to you. Give yourself a big fat permission slip to be you. Honor all parts of you. Don't get caught up in the comparisons.

The thing is, it doesn't matter how cool you look on social media, how pretty your stuff is, or that so and so's stuff is perfect and they have so much and yours isn't. What is more important than all of that is being authentic and getting your energy across and connecting with your ideal client emotionally. That's it. It's the energetic algorithm. It's not about follower amounts or how many likes or comments you received. It's about your voice, relationships, and trust because those are the things that will help you attract your soul aligned community. A soul aligned community, specifically curated with intention, will forever be so much bigger than your follower count or being "cool."

Here is the secret formula:

Your Voice = Content

Content = Relationships

Relationships = Trust

Trust = Soulmate Clients

The first part of the formula is your voice but where your voice comes from is not just you. It's your soul and it's a cocreation with the universe, God, spirit, for what is supposed to come through you so before you create, say this:

Universe, spirit, God (whatever you believe in)

- Please have this reach who it needs to reach

- Please have me share this in the way you want me to

- Please speak through me

- Please allow my truth and energy to come through me

- Please have this capture their attention

When you have the thoughts that people will judge you, people will think you're crazy, and maybe you should delete a certain part. Don't. If you don't say what is on your heart, you are doing a disservice to your true people, the people who are supposed to work with you and the people who vibe with the true you. You legit won't reach them all because you worried about what someone else would think of you. Don't be a best kept secret, be a well-known expert.

Don't be an energetic cock block and stop the clients who are supposed to reach you. Imagine it like you are meeting the universe halfway. Just like you would if you were dating, you can't just expect the person to show up in your driveway, you have to put yourself out there. So do your job of putting your authentic voice out there and let the universe help you out with who it reaches.

Bye, Felicia (To the Keyboard Warriors)

Remember that haters will always exist; they aren't supposed to work with you. It's okay to repel people. You are just saving space and making room for the people who truly do want to work with you. Stay focused on your mission. Your haters don't need to know your mission or understand it, but you need to stay focused on it. I like to say "bye, Felicia" to the keyboard warriors. If someone is truly happy, content with their life and/or business, they won't go out of their way to say something negative to you. Don't let their unhappiness affect your happiness and certainly don't let it affect your business. Send love to the haters and handle it with grace.

Fear

Fear will always be there, and some coaches say to feel the fear and do it anyway, but I disagree. It's not about feeling the fear and doing it anyway. It's about feeling the fear, recognizing the fear, saying hi to it, and having a conversation with it to ultimately release the fear AND THEN go and do the thing. It can look like this, "I see your fear, I understand it's scary to be judged, especially because I've been judged in the past and it left me feeling hurt, but I have a bigger mission here. And it's worth it to me to be judged if it means I'm reaching the people I'm supposed to help because they are looking for me and I have something that can help them. I would be doing a disservice if I didn't help them. So, thank you for trying to protect me, fear. I appreciate you, but I'm going to need you to take a backseat right now. I'm a big girl and I got this. Let me do my thing."

Now fear is gone and it's more feelings of ambition, excitement and being fueled to complete your soul's mission.

There are three ways of creating in this world:

1. **Self-limiting Creating:** Just following other people, holding back creations due to fear.

2. **Co-creating:** Partnering with the universe so you feel supported by life and your creations.

3. **Soul-creating:** Allowing the universe to quite literally create through you, birthing something new and feeling completely supported. Synchronicities happen and you are in flow!

In order to get to the place of soul creating you must align your energy first. After all, all that we are made up of is just energy. If you were to hold your hand out in front of you, it would just look like your hand, but if you were to put your hand under a microscope a million times over, you would see a bunch of light particles zipping around. You would just be seeing energy. We are just energy, that's it.

Energy is everything. The abundance game of life and being able to attract goodness into your life comes from being able to hold your energy and emotions in a high vibrational state.

Dr. David Hawkins went out and measured different emotional states and mapped them out on the scale of consciousness for us. (Cooper, 2022) I'm such a visual learner so this graph changed my life when I understood it.

Review of Dr. Hawkin's "Map of Consciousness" 18 Major Levels

Level #	Level Name	Emotions	Process	Self-View	God-View
1000	Enlightenment	Ineffable	Pure	Is	Self
700			Consciousness		
		enlightened crown chakra radiance halo			
600	Peace	Bliss	Illumination	Perfect	All-Being
		spontaneous healing			
540	Joy	Serenity	Transfiguration	Complete	One
500	Love	Reverence	Revelation	Benign	Loving
400	Reason	Understanding	Abstraction	Meaningful	Wise
350	Acceptance	Forgiveness	Transcendence	Harmonious	Merciful
310	Willingness	Optimism	Intention	Hopeful	Inspiring
250	Neutrality	Trust	Release	Satisfactory	Enabling
200	Courage	Affirmation	Empowerment	Feasible	Permitting

POWER (left side), STRONG (right side)

200 Levels ABOVE 200 Love Truth, Integrity, Support Life   Creative Powers   Lift Up   200

199 Levels BELOW 200 false, deception, prey on Life   destructive forces   pull down   199

clever preditory entanglements

Level #	Level Name	Emotions	Process	Self-View	God-View
175	Pride	Scorn	Inflation	Demanding	Indifferent
150	Anger	Hate	Aggression	Antagonistic	Vengeful
125	Desire	Craving	Enslavement	Disappointing	Denying
100	Fear	Anxiety	Withdrawl	Frightening	Punitive
75	Grief	Regret	Despondence	Tragic	Disdainful
50	Apathy	Despair	Abdication	Hopeless	Condemning
30	Guilt	Blame	Destruction	Evil	Vindictive
20	Shame	Humiliation	Elimination	Miserable	Despising
1	Bacteria				

FORCE (left side), WEAK (right side)

POWER is creative, constructive, self-sustaining, permanent, stationary, energizing and invincible.
FORCE is destructive, temporary, draining, depletes energy, and moves from location to location.

Logarithmic Energy Field increases: $1 = 1$; $2 = 10$; $3 = 100$; $4 = 1,000$; $5 = 10,000$; $6 = 100,000$ ...etc.

All levels below 500 are "objective" and all levels from 500 to 1,000 are "subjective."

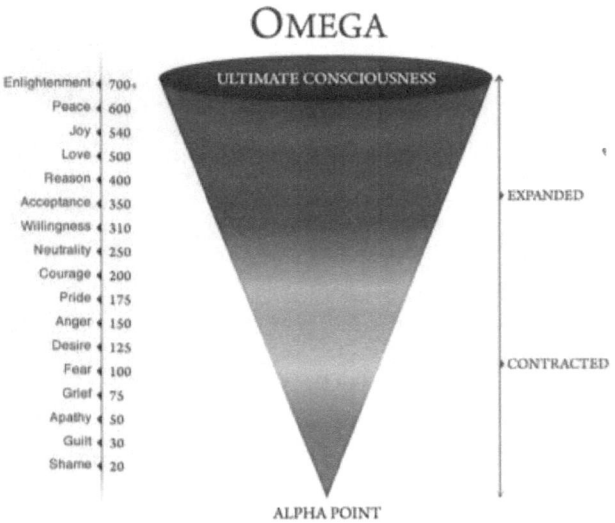

There are contracted and forceful states and then there are expanded and powerful states.

The red color is the lower and slower more dense frequencies, and the purple is the faster, higher vibrating frequencies.

The lower you are on the spectrum, the more you are living in the denser frequencies such as guilt, shame and fear. This makes it really hard to get anything done and it will take a lot of force. In the dense frequencies, it will seem like you are just trying to get through the day, and you will most likely be in a state of fight or flight. You may also attract more guilt, shame, and fear into your life.

Everything works through resonance so wherever you are vibrating on this scale is what you will attract. This is what the law of attraction comes down to. The higher you are on the spectrum the easier things will be for you, you will just be in flow. The goal is to stay as high on the scale as possible. Love and above!

So how do you stay high on the scale, you might ask?

Well, we know that where focus goes energy flows, right? It's all a game of attention. Consciously and deliberately putting your attention where you want it.

With that being said, you need to keep your focus on achieving your goal. We take in 2.3 million bits of information per second. All the thoughts we have are not always ours. They aren't always the truth. If your focus seems to veer away from your goal or the positives, simply do your best to bring your focus back.

Although the goal itself is fun, it's never really about the thing itself. Everything we want is because we think we will feel better in the possession of it. It's really about the emotion that the goal or thing provides us.

In short, you need to ask yourself. "How will I feel when I achieve the thing?" and if it's feelings such as happiness, fulfillment, excitement, awe, love, and so on, then you need to ask yourself how you can bring those feelings into your life right now. You need to feel the feelings first. You need to vibrate high on the scale first, and then and only then will you be an energetic match to welcome that thing or goal into your life. Positivity attracts positivity.

It's your choice. You can either force your way there or you can raise your vibration and state of consciousness and allow those goals and dreams to easily and effortlessly manifest into your life.

Your homework: Get your energy right first, then take inspired action!

Pro tip to get your energy right:

- Journal about it and feel the hype

- Go on a talking rant like you are telling a friend or family member about how much you've accomplished

- Exercise with the intention of working towards it

- Surround yourself with evidence that it's possible

- Visualize it happening

- Practice gratitude

Affirmation: There are opportunities everywhere for me to create abundance and share my message. Everything is an opportunity. I am open. There is enough.

For some reason, we tend to believe that something grand like our dream business, our soulmate, or a luxury five-star vacation is harder to manifest than a cup of coffee. We think that because coffee is so cheap, so commonly found, and so small that it's easy for the universe to bring it to us. Whereas, a 10-day trip to Bora Bora in an overwater bungalow with your sweetie is really hard and will take a lot of time. Let me fill you in on a secret: The energy between the two desires is exactly the same. It's just energy. It doesn't take any longer to manifest one than it does the other. It's all in your head.

Time doesn't exist in the universe. It's a human created concept, therefore, stop creating limits. It's no easier to manifest five dollars than it is to manifest 100 dollars and it doesn't take longer to manifest 100 dollars than it does to manifest five dollars. The amount of energy behind five and 100 dollars is exactly the same. Everything is energy. It's universal law. When you learned about gravity you didn't not believe your teacher and attempt to jump off a cliff, did you? There is no difference here.

If you'd like to learn without the pain of leaping off a cliff, please contact me and my team to book a no cost strategy session so you can learn from an expert the exact steps you need to take start your dream coaching business. Please visit www.carlyhillcoaching.com to book your call!

Once you get your energy right and begin taking inspired and aligned action, your next job is to surrender.

Surrender does not mean giving up. It doesn't mean throwing your hands up in the air and saying, 'it is what is it" or "it will happen when it happens, and if it doesn't happen, oh well." NO. Surrendering is keeping your desires in your heart and releasing the how and when. That is the universe's job, not yours. You wouldn't expect the universe to do your job, would you? Manifestation isn't a solo creation. It's a co-creation. Plus, if you knew how it would happen and when it would happen, that would ruin the surprise anyways. If it's inevitable and it's going to happen, no matter what, why the fuck does it matter when it happens? Trust in divine timing. The universe is not a vending machine. You can't put your order in like it's a Starbucks and expect instant gratification.

When something happens and you don't end up getting exactly what you want, it is not a denial. When you prayed and prayed for something to happen on July 11th, and it's now July 12th and the thing still hasn't happened, it is STILL not a denial. You are never denied what you want. You are never denied your desires. Your desires were put into your heart for a reason, and you wouldn't have these desires if they weren't meant to manifest.

When you feel like you are being denied something, it's actually just a detour. The universe is either asking you to be more clear, work out a limiting belief, or it's simply bringing you something even BETTER. The rule of the game is always, "this or something better." It's like when you ordered your coffee and you're stoked to drink it and then you find out the person in front of you paid for it. It got better. Everything always happens for your highest good; you need to start trusting that any sort of detour is not a sign to give up. Don't give up on your desires. They will eventually manifest.

Get clear on your desires. If you desire freedom, then get clear on your vision next. What is the exact vision of freedom? What do you see, hear, and feel? What does freedom mean to you? What does it look like for you? Then, get your energy right. Feel all the emotions you would as if this life is yours right now. Put your order in for this freedom, keep your energy in check, and do the next best thing you know how to do every damn day.

Take care of yourself. Be a gatekeeper of what you allow in your mind. Challenge those negative beliefs. Take care of your body, too. It's the vessel to your mind. It's the car that is going to get you where you want to go.

Your business will never outgrow your consciousness and your business is only as big as your soul knows it to be.

-Carly Hill

Recap:

People hire coaches for three reasons. They can't do it on their own, they want to do it faster, or they want to follow a proven system.

If you run a business, and you can't master sales then it will cost you your whole business. It's a skill you can build.

It's only normal to have imposter syndrome.

You are sharing your genius. You aren't selling shit. You can't put a price tag on your genius.

Keyboard warriors will always exist, pray for their happiness and move on.

Chapter 6

Do or Die Badass Mindset

Learn how to build a do or die badass mindset so you can scale your coaching business and continue to create a legacy for your family and generations to come. Freedom, flexibility, and security is yours!

Building a successful coaching business requires not only practical skills and knowledge, but also a strong mindset and sense of self-awareness. If you do not do your inner work, you will have a difficult time sustaining your success, growth, and wealth.

Business Mindset > Business Model

Everyone has a different business model and different skill sets but the one thing in common all successful people have is a do or die badass mindset and a willingness to adapt and learn.

"If you can walk, talk, hear or see, you have everything it takes to do something big with your life." – Patrick Bet-David.

I've given you a lot of information in this book and in order for you to go out and apply it, you need to have a strong mindset.

The journey of entrepreneurship is not an easy one and you will be faced with various challenges along the way.

Having a strong and resilient attitude is crucial for you because it shapes how you will approach challenges, take risks, manage stress, and innovate, especially in the face of adversity. A positive and growth-oriented mindset can help you stay focused, motivated, and resilient when faced with the ups and downs.

Bottom Line: Regardless of how much experience you have, your mindset will play a significant role in your success or failure. Even with all the necessary skills and expertise, if you have a negative or limiting mindset, you will struggle to achieve your goals and reach your full potential and I'm not going to let that happen on my watch.

Let's dive in and do some work.

Your Business is a Mirror

Whatever you love, whatever you hate, whatever you're terrified of, it will all show up in your business.

If you want your clients to be decisive with you, are there any areas in your life you can be more decisive on? Do you want clients to pay you on time or quickly? How do you pay for things? Are you late? Do you pay up front? Do you hesitate before you buy something? This is a mirror. Life is a mirror. We need to look at how we are acting in our own life in order to attract the same action into our life. You probably want your clients to invest in themselves, their personal growth, and their health.

Are you doing the same? (Clearly you are if you're reading this book.)

The way you run your business and make decisions, both personally and professionally, will be reflected in your business.

There is No Failure, Only Feedback

Some coaches will tell you to fail harder or fail forward, but I don't believe in failure at all. Yes, sometimes things don't go according to plan, but does that mean you failed? Failure has a strong connotation, and we must be gentle with our words. The language we use to describe our experiences can shape our beliefs and attitudes, and ultimately influence our actions and outcomes.

Using language that focuses on failure, such as saying, "I failed" or "it failed," can reinforce negative beliefs and attitudes that can hold us back. It can lead to a fixed mindset, where we see our abilities and potential as static and limited, rather than something that can be developed and improved.

On the other hand, using language that focuses on growth and learning, such as saying "I learned from that experience" or "I'm still learning and growing," can promote a growth mindset. This mindset is characterized by a belief that our abilities and potential can be developed and improved through effort and learning.

When we view setbacks as failures, we can become demotivated and discouraged, which can make it harder to move forward and achieve our goals. By reframing setbacks as feedback, we can approach challenges with a growth mindset, seeking to learn from our experiences and make improvements where necessary.

For example, if you launch your program and don't get a paying client right away, you might see it as a failure and give up on the idea altogether. However, if you view it as feedback, you can analyze what went wrong and use that information to improve your approach.

So, I challenge you, next time you say you "failed" catch yourself and switch up the story.

Ego plus Intuition

You have two voices that can be heard at any time, ego and intuition. Ego speaks from fear, or fuck everything and run. Intuition speaks from love. Sometimes we can mistake fear for an opportunity, particularly in situations where the fear is associated with a potential change or new experience. It feels safer to go back in the comfort zone and not make the leap. Fear and excitement show up the same way neurologically, so we have to be careful with our discernment. Fear can be a natural response to unfamiliar or uncertain situations, but it can also be a signal that something is important and worth pursuing. In order for you to clearly discern if it is fear, or if something is an opportunity, it will require you to reflect in silence and go within. Fear is instinctive but it is our job to make decisions not based on fear but based on intuition or love.

For example, imagine that you are presented with the opportunity to speak at an event. Your initial response may be fear or anxiety about speaking in front of a bunch of strangers, especially if you have never done it before. However, if you take a closer look at the opportunity, you may realize that it could be a chance to share your message with a larger audience, attract potential clients, build your professional network, or develop your public speaking skills.

In this case, the fear you initially felt could be a sign that the opportunity is significant and could potentially lead to growth and development.

If you want to start your coaching business but you are fearful, ask yourself if this opportunity opens the doors to fulfillment and abundance and am I willing to take the leap, trusting my desires know the way? If the answer is yes, you know what to do next.

Abundance Mindset

There is enough for everyone. There is more than enough to go around. There are enough resources. There are enough people who need help. There is enough room for everyone to be successful. There is enough. Period. End of sentence.

If someone takes a big piece of the pie, that means there is only a little piece left for you, but the world doesn't work this way. There will always be a shit-ton of coaches in this world; the industry is booming but THE WORLD IS NOT A PIE. If a bunch of other people decide to be coaches, it doesn't mean there is no room left for you to be one. Other people's success does not diminish yours. There is enough space for everyone to thrive.

There is abundance everywhere. There is an abundance of air and water. Look outside at a tree and how many leaves it has or at all the blades of grass. Nature is abundant. Look around your room right now; there is money in everything. It's abundant. It's everywhere. People are everywhere. There is seven billion of us in this world. Everything is abundant. Opportunities are abundant.

Say it with me, "I am open to new experiences and taking calculated risks. The world is abundant and I'm here to pursue my passions with confidence and optimism."

Think Long Term and Think Bigger

I know you are here because your goal is to build an online coaching business, but you are actually building something way bigger. You are building an empire, a legacy!

By starting and growing a coaching business, you have the opportunity to create a lasting impact on your clients and the world, while also building a successful business that can support you and your family.

Everything you do in your business impacts others in a positive way. This is one of the main pillars of conscious living. Every action you take in your business can have a ripple effect that extends far beyond your immediate clients. By helping just one person, you can inspire positive change in their life, and that change can then spread to others in their network and beyond.

You're also building a business around your calling, which allows you to enjoy what you do for a living. People pay you for something you enjoy, and you get to change generations! Do you recognize how powerful you are?

That is freaking badass and it's your birthright to stand in this power. This is what you came here to do, and I want you to remember that! Think about all the impact you can make!

Ultimately, building a coaching business with the intention of leaving a positive legacy is a powerful way to align your values and your work. It can give you a sense of purpose and fulfillment that extends far beyond financial success, and it can motivate you to continue to grow and expand your business in new and meaningful ways.

Be a Lifelong Learner

A wise man knows he knows nothing. - Socrates

By acknowledging that there is always more to learn and that our understanding of the world is limited, we open ourselves up to new ideas, perspectives, and ways of thinking. This mindset of constant learning and growth is essential for anyone who wants to succeed in life, whether in business, relationships, or personal development.

In the context of building a coaching business, the idea of being a lifelong learner is especially important. If you are committed to ongoing learning and personal growth, you are better equipped to provide value to your clients, stay ahead of the curve in your industry, and adapt to changing circumstances.

By staying curious, asking questions, and seeking out new information and experiences, you can expand your knowledge and develop a deeper understanding of yourself and the world around you. This can help you to develop more effective coaching strategies, connect with clients on a deeper level, and stay inspired and motivated in your work.

Learning is a privilege and an honor, and it should be embraced and appreciated throughout our lives.

Surround Yourself with Evidence

"Deliberately seek the company of people who influence you to think and act on building the life you desire."- Napoleon Hill

The four-minute-mile was a record that couldn't be broken for decades. Then in less than two months after it was beat, it was beat again with a time of three minutes 58 seconds and then AGAIN three years later. Three runners in the same race ran the mile in less than four minutes.

Our mind can do anything we set it out to do, even what seems to be physically impossible sometimes.

When you find someone out there in the world who already accomplished what it is you're trying to accomplish, there is nothing that can stop you. Surround yourself with success stories, actual people, and as much evidence as you possibly can. What you want is ABSOLUTELY fucking real. It's only a matter of time before you have it in your own hands. Your belief system greatly affects how much your subconscious mind works FOR you rather than against you. By constantly proving yourself right with these examples, you train your subconscious mind to seek out even more reasons that you are RIGHT for believing that you are capable of achieving anything and everything you desire. Train your subconscious mind to learn that whatever you set your mind to, you can accomplish.

These are things I say to myself:

Carly, wake up at seven am to go to the gym. Carly, take a shower right now. Carly, switch the laundry in 10 minutes. Then I actually do it. I don't dilly dally or procrastinate. I take simple tasks that I already planned to do, and I tell myself exactly when I'm going to do them and then I do them.

When we delay the task, we are actually training our mind to not follow through. Scary, right?

However, when you start to obey the simple commands you give yourself, you train your subconscious mind to actually LISTEN to you when it comes to something bigger in other areas of your life!

Rejection

It's only natural in the coaching space. It's just part of the game. Rejection means you put yourself out there in the first place and that is worth celebrating. You took a risk, made a connection, and put yourself out there! Bravo! You can't get rejected if you never share your message or offer. It's important not to take rejection personally. Separate yourself from your business. Don't make it mean something bigger than it is.

It's just as important to see what isn't working as it is to see what is working. If you post something and it gets zero engagement, you know that you most likely do not want to turn that post into a paid ad. You learned from it. If someone doesn't respond to you, it's okay. Maybe they will come back later and maybe they won't. Rejection isn't the end of the world and it's certainly not the end of your business. It's just a part of it. There is no doubt that it can feel discouraging, but if you are being triggered by the rejection time and time again, this is a whole separate problem. I would recommend some inner child work to discover why this frustration and defeat is showing up for you in the way it is. You want to be able to get to the point of non-attachment with the outcome. Meaning if someone says no, it's no sweat, no pressure, and boom, you move on. It's about being adaptable, resilient, and having the tenacity and perseverance to keep going.

There are many ways to avoid rejection, such as having strong communication, marketing, and sales skills, but even with the strongest of skills, rejection will still happen. Rejection can also be a great opportunity to learn and refine the strategies you are implementing. We are always growing and evolving.

Self-sabotage

Self-sabotage can manifest in different ways, such as procrastination, perfectionism, overworking, avoiding tasks, self-doubt, negative self-talk, and focusing on the wrong priorities. If you are struggling with any of this, it will be important for you to develop self-awareness and identify the underlying beliefs and fears that are driving these behaviors.

I don't need to tell you this, you're a therapist, but a friendly reminder can't hurt.

Think of starting your coaching business like starting a garden. Let's pretend you found the perfect spot for your garden, got the soil ready, and carefully prepped your seeds to plant. As time goes on, and you're watering your plants, you start to doubt your gardening abilities and don't think anything will actually sprout. Then you start to water them less and less, forget to pull the weeds, and don't even bother with the fertilizer. As a result, your garden begins to suffer, and you might even abandon the project all together and decide you are a failed gardener. Total self-sabotage.

Just like a garden, your coaching business needs care and attention in order to flourish. It requires consistent effort and self-awareness. If you don't believe deep down that your coaching business will be successful, then you will subconsciously create scenarios to reinforce this construct. It's science and it's exactly how self-sabotage works. This doesn't have to be your story.

If and when you have a doubt or something gets really hard, stay the course and have faith. You will only have something to show for it if you keep going, focus and see it through.

People Pleasing

People pleasing women can sometimes have a difficult time in the coaching space.

They have a tendency to bend over backwards for others at their own expense, which can lead to an unhealthy work-life balance. Implementing boundaries and learning when to say no is crucial. They also have a difficult time being assertive and confident when describing their offers, not to be confused with pushy or aggressive.

People pleasers are conflict avoidant, so this makes perfect sense. They don't want to share what they have to offer in fear of rejection or receiving an objection because then it would create a conflict of sorts. People pleasers also feel like they have to do everything themselves. However, delegation is essential to maintain productivity.

Self-awareness is key when it comes to identifying areas of growth in this arena. If you know your weaknesses, you can work on improving them. Everyone is always a work in progress.

Money Mindset

To master money, you must master the relationship with yourself. Tony Robbins says the biggest thing keeping people from being wealthy is their brain. (Robbins, 2019) I couldn't agree more. Money occurs in numbers and numbers are infinite so to master something that is infinite is hard. It always leaves you with the feeling that you don't have enough. There is this ever elusive "enough" that keeps you grasping for "more," right!?

In order to feel satisfied with money and have a good relationship with money, you have to master yourself and your thoughts around it.

Do you even know what your relationship with money is like? How would you describe it? Are you close? Do you get along? Do you avoid each other? Do you fight? Do you smile when you think about it? How do you feel when you pay bills or spend money? What attitudes do you have towards people who have money?

What about the role money has in your life? How does it help you? What do you use it for? How does it support you? What has it allowed you to do?

If you are not happy with your relationship with money, how money shows up in your life, how you think and talk about money, then it's because your internal operating system needs updating. It's as if your brain is running on old software. You will not create new experiences from a past paradigm.

Many people associate money with freedom, less stress, peace of mind, security, higher status, and so on, but there are plenty of people who have all the money in the world, and they don't feel free. They are completely stressed, they have massive fear that it will run out, or they just project their fear onto something else instead of the money, but the bottom line is money doesn't equal all those things.

Yes, there are plenty of studies on the correlation between money and happiness but the whole point I'm making here is you must first master yourself and your emotions so that you can have a strong and healthy relationship with money. You don't NEED money to feel freedom. You should embrace feeling free already and then money is a great bonus to make you feel even more free. It's like dating. You shouldn't NEED your partner. You should strive to be your best self, first, and then your partner just amplifies you and makes you better.

Money is a Tool

It can buy nice things and experiences and allow us to support people and causes but it can't buy love, connection, happiness, satisfaction, and the feeling of making a difference. Money can enhance happiness, but it can't buy you a meaningful life. Only you can create a meaningful life for yourself.

You can do it the hard way by DIY'ing it or you can do it the easy way by investing in yourself and working with an experienced mentor who can guide you through the process. Either way, the choice is yours. If you want to do it the easy way, contact my team and me at www.carlyhillcoaching.com

Defining Financial Freedom

In my opinion, financial freedom is never having to worry about money, whether you have any or not. You never obsess about money, but you use money as a tool to create or express yourself. It's as if money is an extension of you. When you are financially free, you see opportunities for growth everywhere and ideas about creating more wealth come to you often. You are generous knowing that money is just an energy exchange, and it will come back to you. This is financial freedom.

Fun Exercise: Next time you spend money on something, I want you to imagine where it's going and how it's helping. You buy your groceries, and you imagine paying the bills of the person checking you out or you imagine them cashing their check to buy gas or buy their family a gift. Thank your money as you spend it as it is allowing someone else to be filled with something they need or want.

<u>Common Beliefs in our Culture about Money</u>

- Money is the root of all evil.

- Money can't buy happiness.

- Money is hard to make.

- Money doesn't matter to me.

- Money isn't everything.

- Therapists/healers aren't supposed to want to make money.

No wonder we have messed up beliefs around money. Do you know what your money beliefs are? More importantly, do you know what your money stories are and where they come from? Did your childhood shape the way you think about money?

For example, my mom used to make me hide the shopping bags from my dad, so I subconsciously learned that spending money on things we wanted was bad. I also used to ask my dad why he always seemed to have money and my mom didn't and his answer was always, "Because I don't care about money." I subconsciously learned that if I wanted money, I shouldn't care about it.

What are your money stories and how has it shaped your beliefs and actions today? We know that creating your future starts with your beliefs, emotions, attitude, and thoughts! Life doesn't happen to you. You create your life based on your internal state. Your internal state and beliefs will determine whether you attract or repel money.

Bad Example

Belief: Money is hard to make.

Emotion: Frustrated, defeated, hopeless

Attitude: Annoyed at others who have money, life isn't fair

Thoughts: No one will buy my program; people can't afford it.

Good Example:

Belief: I make money easily

Emotion: gratitude, excitement

Attitude: open to endless opportunities

Thoughts: People are looking for my program, they want it yesterday

In order to shift your money beliefs, you will need to switch your perception around money. Perception is reality and this means you must stop identifying with the old you and the old money beliefs you used to have. Instead, it needs to be based on what is possible for you and your desired vision. Surround yourself with as much evidence as possible that your desired vision can happen. Other people have achieved it and so can you. Pretend like you are introducing yourself to someone in three years. What do you say? What have you achieved? What does your wealth look like?

Ask yourself, how can I show up as my future self every single day? Try to switch around as much as you can so that your everyday actions align with future you.

Be the wealthy woman now and know why you want to be her. Are you wanting to leave a legacy? Make a larger impact? Go on more adventures? Have financial security? Give back? Have more time and location freedom? Enjoy health and wellness pursuits?

What is your driving factor?

You are Exactly Where You are Supposed to Be

My husband's favorite thing to say is everyone is on their own timeline, and I firmly believe that. You are exactly where you are supposed to be right now, I promise.

Competition is just a made-up story in our head so don't compare yourself to anyone else and their timeline. When you are meant to create something, you will. Some people do things fast. Some do it slow. However, everyone always gets it done if it's a desire. Desires don't let us down. They are seeds planted in our heart for a reason. Anything can happen if you keep at it and believe you can do it. Sounds cliché, I know, but if you do one thing, just keep moving. If someone is doing something fast or doing something slow, they are both still in action and motion. So don't give up and keep moving.

If you ever feel confused or frozen and find yourself stating, "I don't know how" or "I'm stuck," you could be subconsciously protecting yourself from trying something new or failing.

Determination and focus will help you get unstuck. Moving on to something else and distracting yourself with social media, Netflix, or alcohol will not help you get unstuck and will only lead you back to self-sabotage. If you truly are stuck, reach out for help. This is why people hire coaches. Investing in yourself and your business will help you move forward with ease.

Regardless of how you feel, reflect on how far you have come and celebrate the accomplishments and progress you have made. None of us have the same background, privilege, education, or exposure. Everyone is on a different timeline and your timeline is just perfect. Remember five years ago when you dreamed of the things that are happening in your life right now?

Keep your eye on the prize and keep moving forward but never ever forget to look back on how far you have come. Appreciate your growth and all the people who have been and will continue to be a part of it.

Chapter 7
Conclusion

If there was ever a time to be more, make more, and impact more, the time is NOW.

Imagine the days where you don't have to fight with insurance companies or do a bunch of administrative work and notes.

Imagine location freedom and vacations.

Imagine getting paid while you sleep instead of only when your butt is in the uncomfortable therapy chair for 8 hours!

Imagine a sky's the limit mindset where you have paid all your student loans back and still have plenty left over for retirement, your kids college, and fun in the sun!

I want this for you.

No more playing small. I give you permission to go after your dreams right now.

It's time to step into the role of a true Therapreneur™. Be the woman who has it all and leads her clients through life changing transformations.

Entrepreneurship is a wild journey all about innovation. It's a true gift and skill to turn a thought or idea into reality. It takes determination, creativity, belief, and skill. I know you have what it takes within you.

If you don't want to get bogged down with all of the hurdles and challenges standing between you and success, my team and I would be honored to guide you on this Therapreneur™ journey! Contact us at www.carlyhillcoaching.com for your no cost strategy session to lay out your customized coaching blueprint!

I hope this book enlightened you to the endless possibilities you have as an agent of change. It takes a tribe of people, just like you, to make this world a better place. You got a special calling to do this special work and special people don't belong under rocks; they belong on mountain tops. I'd be honored to be your guide to help you get to the top of that mountain.

I am so grateful for your attention, as I know you could have been reading a million other things. So, from the bottom of my heart, thank you. I am always rooting for you. My love is with you.

XOXO Carly Hill

References

Cialdini, R. B. (2021). *Influence the psychology of Persuasion*. Harper Business.

Cooper, J. D. (2022, December 13). *What David Hawkins taught us about the emotional scale of consciousness and achieving higher levels...* Medium. Retrieved March 21, 2023, from https://medium.com/readers-digests/what-david-hawkins-taug ht-us-about-the-emotional-scale-of-consciousness-and-achie ving-higher-levels-a21b337b534d

Godin, S. (2017 July 12). In search of the minimum viable audience. Seth's Blog.

Hormozi, A. (2021). *100M offers. how to make offers so good people feel stupid saying no*. Acquistion.com.

Johnson, B. (2021, February 9). *What's changed with Social Proof in 2019?* IMPACT Inbound Marketing Agency. Retrieved March 21, 2023, from https://www.impactplus.com/blog/whats-changed-with-social -proof-in-2019

Kim, W. C., & Mauborgne Renelle. (2015). *Blue Ocean Strategy: How to create uncontested market space and make the competition irrelevant.* Harvard Business Review Press.

Lahmi, Z. (2022, December 28). *Nail your sales funnel in 6 steps.* monday.com Blog. Retrieved March 21, 2023, from https://monday.com/blog/crm-and-sales/sales-funnel/

Laja, P. (2022, December 26). *Purchase decisions: 9 things that influence consumer decision process.* CXL. Retrieved March 21, 2023, from https://cxl.com/blog/9-things-to-know-about-influencing-purc hasing-decisions/

Robbins, Tony (2019). *Unshakeable: Your guide to financial freedom.* Simon & Schuster.

Stafford, L. (2017, July 13). *Council post: How to incorporate video into your Social Media Strategy.* Forbes. Retrieved March 21, 2023, from https://www.forbes.com/sites/yec/2017/07/13/how-to-incorpor ate-video-into-your-social-media-strategy/?sh=222530a87f2e

Wadhwan, P., & Gankar, S. (2022, April 29). *Elearning market size worth $1 TN by 2028.* Global Market Insights Inc. Retrieved March 21, 2023, from https://www.gminsights.com/pressrelease/elearning-market

What is social proof? definition by dynamic yield. Dynamic Yield. (2020, November 13). Retrieved March 21, 2023, from https://www.dynamicyield.com/glossary/social-proof/

Acknowledgements:

Thank you to the entire team of Elite Coach Group™ for providing the opportunity for me to write this book and guiding me to be the most successful mentor possible.

Thank you to the entire team of All Write Well for helping me throughout the process of writing, editing, and publishing this book. It wouldn't have come to life without you.

Thank you to my parents for always being my number one supporter and believing in me.

Thank you to my husband and friends for understanding when I said "No, I can't. I have to finish my book."

Thank you to wine, sparkling water, and candles for always being by my side as I spent countless hours pouring my heart and soul into this book.

Most importantly, thank you to my spirit team for always having my back and divinely guiding me in this beautiful life of mine.

And lastly, thank you to YOU for buying this book and taking the time to read it.

About the Author:

Carly Hill is a licensed clinical social worker and business strategist for female clinicians. She specializes in helping female therapists make more money and impact by teaching them to build the online coaching business of their dreams.

Carly helps therapists break free out of the one-on-one model to leverage their time, get paid for their knowledge, and live a life of true freedom. She helps therapists to find their coaching niche, develop their high-ticket offer, and organically call in their ideal clients easily and effortlessly using her unique modern marketing masterplan.

When you don't find Carly at the gym, in the Bahamas, or coaching other clinicians, you can find her donating her time to healing others. She is a Reiki master, intuitive, and conscious leader in her community. Gratitude is the number one value she lives her life by.

About the Business:

Carly Hill Coaching LLC was created to help ambitious, driven, and intentional therapists outgrow the office, make a larger impact, and monetize their gifts and skills so they earn back the freedom, flexibility, and security they deserve.

Our signature program, Therapist to Coach Accelerator™ is our high-level training program that was carefully developed for skilled therapists who are ready to quickly start and grow their online coaching business with a proven system and strategy and with guidance, support, and accountability every step of the way. This program is perfect for therapists looking to learn how to add coaching legally and ethically as well as create, market, sell, and deliver their first signature coaching program.

Our clients get access to top level support, customized feedback, detailed reviews, done for you templates, and insider marketing and sales secrets to attract ideal clients and build the coaching business of their dreams.

To learn more please visit our website or email us.

https://www.carlyhillcoaching.com/

hello@carlyhillcoaching.com

Connect with Me:

Website:
https://www.carlyhillcoaching.com

Facebook Group:
https://www.facebook.com/groups/carlyhillcoaching

Facebook Page:
https://www.facebook.com/carlyhillcoaching

Instagram:
https://www.instagram.com/carlyhillcoaching